Knitting at Home

60 Classics from Ella Rae Designs

LEANNE PROUSE

Sixth&Spring Books
161 Avenue of the Americas,
New York, NY 10013
sixthandspringbooks.com

Managing Editor
WENDY WILLIAMS

Senior Editor
MICHELLE BREDESON

Art Director
SHERYL STEPHENS

Instructions Editor and Proofreader
LEANNE PROUSE

Copy Editor
ERIN SLONAKER

Technical Illustrations
SHERYL STEPHENS

Photography
ACORN PHOTO
Other photography by
CAROL JONES pages 34, 39–43
ROD VERVEST page 46 (Lighthouse)
LISA THOMPSON pages 118–122

Vice President, Publisher
TRISHA MALCOLM

Production Manager
DAVID JOINNIDES

President
ART JOINNIDES

Library of Congress Control Number: 2010929567
ISBN: 978-1-933027-99-9
Manufactured in China   3 5 7 9 10 8 6 4
First Edition

Knitting at Home *Contents*

What could be more indulgent than relaxing on the couch and flipping through a gorgeous book, getting lost in its pages, inspired to pick up the knitting needles and start that project that jumps off the page and captures your heart?

Knitting at Home

This book is a compilation of all the things that I love, a passion for textiles, yarn, fabric, embroidery, textures, prints, color—everything tactile and aesthetically pleasing.

How could I resist the opportunity to combine all the things that I love to surround myself with, making it more than a knitting book—a book to stimulate the reader into creating things for the home, things that they can proudly put on display and soak up the admiration from visitors, things that have been "made with love".

Knitting at Home takes us on a journey through the home, showing how knitting can be incorporated into the decor of any room, from practical things to be used every day, like the set of place mats, to the fun and quirky that might only be used on occasion, like the egg cozies and cup warmers. The Intarsia Floor Pillow, inspired by passionfruit flowers and Indian embroidery, will become a focal point of any room, bursting with beautiful colors.

Let your creativity flow and have some fun with projects like the little doll set—Madeleine and Jaqueline—a perfect gift that a little girl will treasure. Cozy up in comfortable knits created especially for lazy days when the weather turns cool, while you knit some favorite socks or a snug wrap cardigan.

It's the simple things in life that sometimes give the greatest pleasure: the joy of sharing good times with family and friends, and the satisfaction of making your house a comfortable and inviting home for those that share it with you. Welcome to *Knitting at Home*—truly something worth staying in for.

A Room for Living

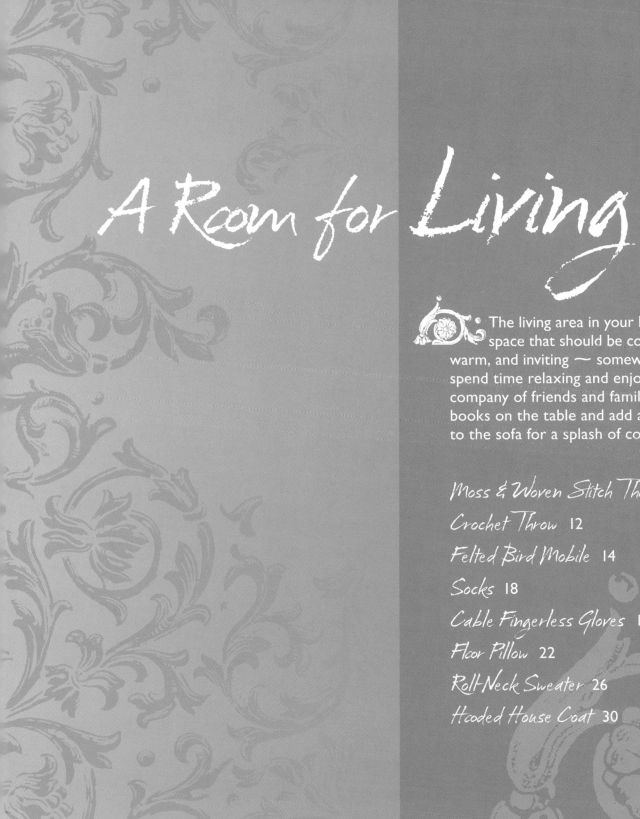

The living area in your home is a space that should be comfortable, warm, and inviting ~ somewhere to spend time relaxing and enjoying the company of friends and family. Lay books on the table and add a throw to the sofa for a splash of color.

MOSS & WOVEN STITCH THROW

A challenging project for an experienced knitter, the woven stitch pattern is very robust and durable.

YARN Ella Rae CLASSIC		
100g/3.5oz	200m/219yds	
Col.	No.	Quantity x 100g balls
col A	03	4
col B	17	3
col C	21	2
col D	23	2

MEASUREMENTS
Width approx 100cm (39½in)
Length approx 150cm (59in)
NEEDLES
1 pair 4.50mm (US 7) needles.
TENSION/GAUGE
21 sts and 26 rows measured over 10cm (4in)
of Woven st using 4.50mm (US 7) needles.

Moss St
Row 1 K1 * p1, k1; rep from * to end.
Rep this row.

Woven St Pattern
Row 1 (RS) K1 * yf, sl 1, yb, k1; rep from * to end.
Row 2 Purl.
Row 3 K2, * yf, sl 1, yb, k1; rep from * to last st, k1.
Row 4 Purl.
These 4 rows form patt rep.

Color Sequence
** Work 2 rows col B, 2 rows col C,
2 rows col B, 3 rows col A, 2 rows col D, 3 rows col A. ***
These 14 rows form color sequence.

THROW
Using 4.50mm (US 7) needles and col A, cast on 215 sts.
Work in Moss st until length measures 4cm (1½in),
ending on a WS row.
(RS) Work 7 sts in col A and Moss st, work row 1 of
Woven st pattern in repeat to last 7 sts, work 7 sts in
Moss st and col A.
(WS) Work 7 sts in col A and Moss st, work row 2 of
Woven st pattern in repeat to last 7 sts, work 7 sts in
col A and Moss st.
These 2 rows set the pattern with a border of Moss st in
col A throughout.
Cont working in pattern as set, working the color
sequence in repeat throughout until length measures
approx 146cm (57½in) finishing on a full repeat of the
color sequence.
Work 4cm (1½in), of Moss st in col A, ending on a
WS row. Cast off.
Press using a warm iron over a damp cloth. ❏

There is something special about creating things for your home, about making a space your own comfort zone with handcrafted pieces made with love.

Moss and Woven Stitch Throw

When fall approaches, it's time to bring out your earth-toned yarns. These colors will add warmth to your home.

Felted Bird Mobile

Crochet Throw

CROCHET THROW

This crochet throw is worked in squares and sewn together.

YARN Ella Rae CLASSIC		
100g/3.5oz 200m/219yds		
Col.	No.	Quantity x 100g balls
col A	23	4
col B	27	2
col C	11	2

MEASUREMENTS
Width approx 96cm (37¾in)
Length approx 110cm (43¼in)

NEEDLES
1 4.50mm crochet hook (US G).

CROCHET ABBREVIATIONS
dc (double crochet)–Insert hook into sts, yo hook, draw through st. (2 loops on hook). Yo, draw through 2 loops on hook (1 loop on hook). St completed.
dbl tr (double treble)–Yo twice, insert hook into st. Yo, draw loop through st. (4 loops on hook). Yo, draw through 2 loops on hook (3 loops on hook). Yo, draw through 2 loops on hook (2 loops on hook). Yo, draw through rem loops (1 loop on hook). St completed.

THROW

Squares

10 ch, join in a ring with a sl.st.
Round 1 10 ch., * [4 dbl tr, 7 ch] 3 times into ring, 3 dbl tr, sl st to 3rd st of first 10 ch, sl st over 3 sts and turn work.
Round 2 10 dc, miss 1 st, along each side, join with a sl.st.
Round 3 10 ch, [2 dbl tr into 1st dc, 1 dbl tr into each of next 8 dc, 2 dbl tr into next dc, 7 ch] 3 times, 2 dbl tr into 1st dc of next 10 dc, 1 dbl tr into each of next 9 dc, sl.st. to 3rd ch of first 10 ch and sl st over 3 sts, turn work.
Round 4 Work as round 2, working 18 dc on each side instead of 10.
Round 5 3 ch, work 1 dbl tr in each st and 6 into each corner.
Fasten off.

Make 18 squares col A, 9 squares col B and 9 squares col C. Using col A work 1 round of dc around each square. (36 squares)

Using edge to edge st OR crochet, join in rows as follows:
Row 1 Col C, col A, col B, col A, col C, col A.
Row 2 Col A, col B, col A, col C, col A, col B.
Row 3 Col B, col A, col C, col A, col B, col A.
Row 4 Col A, col C, col A, col B, col A, col C.
Row 5 Col C, col A, col B, col A, col C, col A.
Row 6 Col A, col B, col A, col C, col A, col B.

Press using a warm iron over a damp cloth. ❏

Handy Tip

I was inspired by the delicate warm tones of fall for this charming throw. It would also look good in different tones of green or blue.

My grandmother taught me how to crochet when I was about ten years old.

FELTED BIRD MOBILE

A delightful and simple felting project that uses basic embroidery skills.

YARN	Ella Rae CLASSIC		
100g/3.5oz	200m/219yds		
Col	No.	Quantity x 100g balls
col A	27	1
col B	11	1
col C	23	1
Small length of red yarn.		

MEASUREMENTS
Each bird 12cm (4¾in) x 7cm (2¾in)

NEEDLES
1 pair 4.50mm (US 7) needles.

TENSION/GAUGE
20 sts and 24 rows measured over10cm (4in) of St st using 4.50mm (US 7) needles.

ADDITIONAL REQUIREMENTS
Embroidery needle
Embroidery thread
10 small beads
30 large glass beads
Bell
Polyester Fiberfill

Piece 1

Using 4.50mm (US 7) needles and col A, cast on 45 sts.
Work in St st until length measures approx 30cm (11¾in). Cast off.

Piece 2

Make another piece the same size as piece 1, using col B.

Piece 3

Using 4.50mm (US 7) needles and col C, cast on 45 sts.
Work in St st until length measures approx 15cm (6in). Cast off.

MAKING UP

Double felt all pieces separately (see method on page 152).
Using the template on page 151, cut out 4 from piece 1, 4 from piece 2 and 2 from piece 3.
Sew 2 pieces tog along edge from head to tail.
Make a cord using the 3 colors plus a strand of red thread, braided tog until approx 90cm (35½in) in length.
Thread cord onto embroidery needle, tie a knot in cord approx 10cm (4in) from end. Thread 5 large glass beads onto cord.
Insert cord through center of base of first bird, sliding bird down cord to sit on top of beads.
Insert Polyester Fiberfill between the 2 pieces of bird and sew along top edge.
Note: It is easier to thread cord through birds before they are filled.
Rep this process for each bird.
Tie a loop at top of cord for hanging.
Tie bell to bottom of cord.
Sew on small beads for eyes.
Embroider birds—see photo for embroidery design.
Sew small tufts of red yarn onto tail. ❏

Handy Tip

It is the small treasures we make to decorate our home that say so much about who we are. Personalize your own mobile by selecting colors to work with your decor.

Handpainted Portuguese
ceramics inspired this
mobile of felted and
embroidered birds.

A house is a dwelling that offers shelter. A home is where you express yourself.

Socks

SOCKS

These simple socks are a great project for the "novice" sock knitter.

YARN Ella Rae CLASSIC HEATHERS
100g/3.5oz   200m/219yds
Col. No.   Quantity x 100g balls
123   2
MEASUREMENTS
Size fits average adult.
NEEDLES
1 pair 4.50mm (US 7) needles.

TENSION/GAUGE
20 sts and 24 rows measured over 10cm (4in) of St st using 4.50mm (US 7) needles.

SOCKS

Loosely cast on 40 sts. Divide sts onto 3 needles. (13-14-13)
Round 1 * K2, p2; rep from * to end.
Rep this round for 5cm (2in).
Next round Knit.
Rep this round until length (incl band) measures 20cm (8in).
Heel Knit the first 10 sts of round onto one needle, slip the last 10 sts of round onto other end of same needle.
(These 20 sts are for the heel)
Divide rem sts onto two needles and leave for instep.
Work 13 rows on heel sts in alt rows of purl and knit.
To turn heel
K13, k2tog, k1, turn.
P8, p2tog, p1, turn.
K9, k2tog, k1, turn.
P10, p2tog, p1, turn.
K11, k2tog, k1, turn.
All sts are now worked onto one needle. (15 sts)
Purl back 7 of these sts. (Heel complete)
Slip all instep sts onto one needle.
Using another needle, with RS facing, k7 heel sts, then pick up and k10 sts along side of heel. With a second needle, k across instep sts. With 3rd needle, pick up and k10 sts along other side of heel, then k8 rem heel sts. (55 sts)
Dec for instep
Round 1 Knit.
Round 2 1st needle—k to last 4 sts, k2tog, k2.
2nd needle—knit.
3rd needle—k2, sl 1, k1, psso, k to end.

Rep these 2 rounds 6 times more.
Cont without shaping until foot length measures 22cm (8¾in) (or length desired) from side of heel where sts were knitted up.
Shape toe
Round 1 1st needle—k to last 3 sts, k2tog, k1.
2nd needle—k1, sl 1, k1, psso, k to last 3 sts, k2tog, k1.
3rd needle—k1, sl 1, k1, psso, k to end.
Rep this round until 13 sts rem.
Work 1 round without shaping, then 1st needle of next round.
Slip sts on 3rd needle onto end of 1st needle.
Graft or darn sts tog. ❏

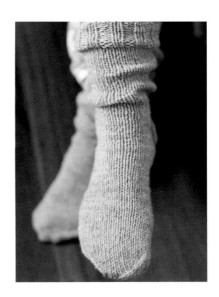

CABLE FINGERLESS GLOVES

These fingerless gloves are an easy cable project.

YARN Ella Rae AMITY
100g/3.5oz   182m/200yds

Col. No.	Quantity x 100g balls
2	1

NEEDLES
1 pair 4.50mm (US 7) needles.
1 pair 5.00mm (US 8) needles.

TENSION/GAUGE
18 sts and 24 rows measured over 10cm (4in) of St st using 5.00mm (US 8) needles.

SPECIAL ABBREVIATIONS
C4F or C4B (Cable 4 Front or Cable 4 Back) slip next 2 sts onto cable needle and hold at front (or back) of work, knit next 2 sts from left-hand needle, then knit sts from cable needle.

CABLE PATTERN

Row 1 Knit.
Row 2 (and all WS rows) Purl.
Row 3 * K2, C4B; rep from * to end.
Row 5 Knit.
Row 7 * C4F, k2; rep from * to end.
Row 8 Purl.
These 8 rows form pattern repeat.

RIGHT GLOVE

Using 5.00mm (US 8) needles, cast on 42 sts.
Cont working in Cable Pattern repeat
until length measures 20cm (8in), ending on a WS row.
Change to 4.50mm (US 7) needles.
Cont working in k2, p2 rib until length measures 23cm (9in) from beg, ending on a WS row. Cast off in rib.

LEFT GLOVE

Work as for right glove.

MAKING UP

Press pieces gently using a warm iron over a damp cloth.
Sew seam, leaving an opening for the thumb approx 2cm (¾in) wide just above beginning of rib. ❏

Handy Tip

Cable knitting for beginners: start with a simple pattern and experience the joys of making something very special.

Nature offers us so much inspiration. Vines bursting with new life in spring and exotic passionfruit flowers have inspired this beautiful intarsia floor pillow.

Floor Pillow

FLOOR PILLOW

Intarsia and embroidered floor pillow.

YARN Ella Rae CLASSIC		
100g/3.5oz	200m/219yds	
Col. No.	**Quantity x 100g balls**	
col A 59	7	
139	1	
46	1	
98	1	

Yarn for embroidery, col no's:
56, 78, 80, 98, 99.

MEASUREMENTS
Width 85cm (33½in)
Length 75cm (29½in)

NEEDLES
1 4.50mm (US 7) circular needle.

ADDITIONAL REQUIREMENTS
1 darning needle
1 90cm (35½in) pillow insert

TENSION/GAUGE
20 sts and 24 rows measured over 10cm (4in) of St st using 4.50mm (US 7) needles.

NOTE A circular needle is used to hold the large number of sts, rows are worked back and forth, not in rounds.

FRONT
Using 4.50mm (US 7) needles and col A, cast on 156 sts.
Working St st, refer to graph on page 146 for pattern placement and color changes.
Work 200 graph rows.
Cast off.

BACK
Using 4.50mm (US 7) needles and col A, cast on 156 sts.
Work in St st until length measures same as front, ending on a WS row.
Cast off.

MAKING UP
Press pieces gently, using a warm iron over a damp cloth.
Embroider pillow, using guide on page 147.

Sew front and back pieces tog along 3 sides using edge to edge st (or method preferred).
Slip pillow insert into place and sew rem edge. ❏

Create this special floor pillow for your favorite sunny spot to sit and ponder.

Handy Tips

When working intarsia patterns *it is often messy and awkward working from a number of different colors. To avoid this problem, wind off enough yarn for each section of color onto a bobbin or piece of card.*

Reading Charts: *Make an enlarged photocopy of the chart and mark off each row as it is completed. Work knit rows from right to left and purl rows left to right.*

Knitting is a joyous skill. Like many crafts, knitting is a skill we take with us on our journey through life and pass on to following generations.

Roll-Neck Sweater

ROLL-NECK SWEATER

An easy sweater to knit and wear. Loose and comfortable for carefree days.

YARN Ella Rae CLASSIC HEATHERS

100g/3.5oz   200m/219yds

	A	B	C	D	
Bust	80	90	100	110	cm
	31½	35½	39½	43¼	in

Col. No.	Quantity x 100g balls			
135	6	7	8	9

MEASUREMENTS

Refer to diagram on page 148.

NEEDLES

1 pair 4.00mm (US 6) needles.

1 pair 4.50mm (US 7) needles.

1 4.00mm (US 6) circular needle.

TENSION/GAUGE

20 sts and 24 rows measured over 10cm (4in) of St st using 4.50mm (US 7) needles.

BACK and FRONT

Using 4.00mm (US 6) needles, cast on 113(123,133,143) sts.

(RS) K1 * p1, k1; rep from * to end.

(WS) P1 * k1, p1; rep from * to end.

These 2 rows form rib.

Work 8cm (3¼in) in rib, ending on a RS row.

Change to 4.50mm (US 7) needles.

Cont working in St st, beg with a knit row until length (incl band) measures 36cm (14¼in), ending on a WS row.

Shape armholes (RS) Cast off 6 sts at beg next 2 rows. [101(111,121,131) sts]

Next row (RS) (dec) Dec 1 st each end next row, then 1 st each end foll alt rows 5 times more. [89(99,109,119) sts]

Cont working in St st until length (incl band) measures 44(45,46,47) cm [17¼(17¾,18,18½) in], ending on a WS row.

Shape neck (RS) Patt 38(42,46,50) sts, turn, leave rem sts on a holder. Work each side of neck separately.

(WS) P2tog, p to end.

(RS) K to last 2 sts, k2tog.

Rep last 2 rows 8 times more, then WS row again. [19(23,27,31) sts, 19 shaping rows]

Cont working straight until length measures 56(57,58,59) cm [22(22½,22¾,23¼) in], ending on a WS row.

Shape shoulder (RS) Cast off 6(8,9,10) sts at beg next row, then beg foll alt row once.

Purl 1 row.

Cast off rem 7(7,9,11) sts.

With RS facing, rejoin yarn to rem sts, cast off 13(15,17,19) center sts, k to end.

(WS) P to last 2 sts, p2tog.

(RS) K2tog, k to end.

Rep last 2 rows 8 times more, the WS row again. [19(23,27,31) sts, 19 shaping rows]

Cont working straight until length measures 56(57,58,59) cm [22(22½,22¾,23¼) in], ending on a RS row.

Shape shoulder (WS) Cast off 9(10,12,13) sts, at beg next row, then beg foll alt row once.

Purl 1 row.

Cast off rem 7(7,9,11) sts.

SLEEVES

Using 4.00mm (US 6) needles, cast on 66(68,70,72) sts.

Work in k1, p1 rib as back and front until length measures 8cm (3¼in), ending on a WS row.

Change to 4.50mm (US 7) needles.

Cont working in St st, AT THE SAME TIME **shape sides** as foll:

Inc 1 st each end foll 11th row once, then 1 st each end foll 16th rows 4 times more.

[76(78,80,82) sts, 75 shaping rows]

Cont working straight until length (incl band) measures 42cm (16½in), ending on a WS row.

Shape sleeve top (RS) Cast off 6 sts at beg next 2 rows. [64(66,68,70) sts]

Next row (RS) (dec) Dec 1 st each end next row, then 1 st each end foll alt rows 4(5,6,7) times. (54 sts)

Purl 1 row.

(RS) Cast off 3 sts at beg next 6 rows, then 2 sts at beg foll 10 rows. (16 sts) Cast off rem sts.

MAKING UP

Press pieces gently on WS, using a warm iron over a damp cloth.

Join shoulder seams. Sew side seams.

Sew sleeve seams. Center sleeves into armhole, sew into position.

Neckband With RS facing, using 4.00mm (US 6) circ needle, beg at left shoulder seam, pick up and knit 84(88,92,96) sts along front neck and 84(88,92,96) sts along back neck. [168(176,184,192) sts]

Work in rounds of k1, p1 rib until length measures 8cm (3¼in), ending at left shoulder seam.

Next round (dec) * K3tog, rib 5; rep from * 21(22,23,24) times. [126(132,138,144) sts]

Work a further 8cm (3¼in) in k1, p1 rib. Cast off in rib. ❏

When you decorate your home with handcrafted objects, throws and cushions, housework becomes an opportunity to appreciate their unique beauty.

Hooded House Coat 29

HOODED HOUSE COAT

This easy-fit house coat is so comfortable you will want to live in it.

YARN Ella Rae CLASSIC HEATHERS
100g/3.5oz 200m/219yds

	S–M	L–XL	
Bust	80–100	110–130	cm
Col. No.	Quantity x 100g balls		
139	9	11	

NEEDLES
1 pair 4.50mm (US 7) needles.

MEASUREMENTS
Refer to diagram on page 148.

TENSION/GAUGE
20 sts and 24 rows measured over 10cm (4in) of St st using 4.50mm (US 7) needles.

SPECIAL ABBREVIATIONS
Dec right Sl 1, k1, psso, put st back onto left needle, bring second st on left needle over first st, put st back onto right needle.

BACK

Using 4.50mm (US 7) needles, cast on 105(121) sts.
Cont working in St st, beg with a knit row, until length measures 50cm (19¾in), ending on a WS row.
Shape raglan armholes (RS) Cast off 6 sts at beg next 2 rows. [93(109) sts]
Next row (RS) [K1, p1] 3 times, k to last 6 sts, [p1,k1] 3 times.
(WS) [P1, k1] 3 times, p to last 6 sts, [K1, p1] 3 times.
Next row (RS) (dec) [K1, p1] 3 times, dec right, k to last 9 sts, sl 1, k2tog, psso, [P1, k1] 3 times.
Cont working as set, dec 2 sts each end of foll 6th row once, then on every foll 4th row, 12(14) times. [37(45) sts]
Work 3 rows. Cast off rem sts.

LEFT FRONT

Using 4.50mm (US 7) needles, cast on 52(60) sts.
Cont working in St st until length measures same as back to armhole shaping,** ending on a WS row.
Shape raglan armhole (RS) Cast off 6 sts, k to end. [46(54) sts]
Work 1 row.
Next row (RS) [K1, p1] 3 times, k to end.
(WS) P to last 6 sts, [K1, p1] 3 times.
Next row (RS) (dec) [K1, p1] 3 times, dec right, k to end.
Cont working as set, dec 2 sts on foll 6th row once, then on every foll 4th row, 8(10) times. [26(30) sts]
Work 3 rows.
Shape front neck (RS) [K1, p1] 3 times, dec right, k7(11) sts, turn, leave rem 10 sts on a holder. [14(18) sts]
(WS) Cast off 2(3) sts, p to last 6 sts, [K1, p1] 3 times. [12(15) sts]
(RS) [K1, p1] 3 times, k to end.
(WS) Cast off 2(3) sts, p to last 6 sts, [K1, p1] 3 times. [10(12) sts]
(RS) [K1, p1] 3 times, dec right, k1(3) sts. [8(10) sts]
(WS) Cast off 2(2) sts, [K1, p1] twice, k1. [6(8) sts]
(RS) [K1, p1] 3 times, k0(2) sts. [6(8) sts]
(WS) **S–M** [K1, p1] 3 times, **L–XL** Cast off 2 sts, [P1, k1] twice, p1. (6 sts)

(RS) [K1, p1] 3 times.
(WS) Cast off 2 sts, p1, k1, p1. (4 sts)
(RS) [K1, p1] twice.
(WS) [K1, p1] twice.
Cast off.

RIGHT FRONT

Work as for left front to **, ending on a RS row.
Shape raglan armhole (WS) Cast off 6 sts, p to end. [46(54) sts]
Next row (RS) K to last 6 sts, [P1, k1] 3 times.
(WS) [P1, k1] 3 times, p to end.
Next row (RS) (dec) K to last 9 sts, sl 1, k2tog, psso, [P1, k1] 3 times.
Cont working as set, dec 2 sts on foll 6th row once, then on every foll 4th row, 8(10) times. [26(30) sts]
Work 2 rows.
Shape front neck (WS) [P1, k1] 3 times, p10(14) sts, turn, leave rem 10 sts on a holder. [14(18) sts]
(RS) Cast off 2(3) sts, k to last 9 sts, sl 1, k2tog, psso, [K1, p1] 3 times. [12(15) sts]
(WS) [P1, k1] 3 times, p to end.
(RS) Cast off 2(3) sts, k to last 6 sts, [P1, k1] 3 times. [10(12) sts]
(WS) [P1, k1] 3 times, p to end.
(RS) K1, sl 1, k2tog, psso, [P1, k1] 3 times. [8(10) sts]
(WS) [K1, p1] 3 times, p to end.
(RS) Cast off 2(2) sts, [K1, p1] twice, k1. [6(8) sts]
(WS) [P1, k1] 3 times.

(RS) S–M [K1, p1] 3 times, L–XL Cast off 2 sts, [P1, k1] twice, p1. (6 sts)
(WS) [P1, k1] 3 times.
(RS) Cast off 2 sts, k1, p1, k1. (4 sts)
(WS) [P1, k1] twice.
(RS) [P1, k1] twice.
Cast off.

SLEEVES

Using 4.50mm (US 7) needles, cast on 61(65) sts.
Cont working in St st, AT THE SAME TIME, **shape sides** as foll:
Inc 1 st each end foll 5th row once, then 1 st each end foll 16th(12th) rows, 6(8) times. [75(83) sts, 101 shaping rows]
Cont working straight until length measures 46cm (18in), ending on a WS row.
Shape raglan (RS) Cast off 6 sts at beg next 2 rows. [63(71) sts]
Next row (RS) [K1, p1] 3 times, k to last 6 sts, [P1, k1] 3 times.
(WS) [P1, k1] 3 times, p to last 6 sts, [K1, p1] 3 times.
Next row (RS) (dec) [K1, p1] 3 times, dec right, k to last 9 sts, sl 1, k2tog, psso, [P1, k1] 3 times. [59(67) sts]
Cont working as set, dec 2 sts each end foll 6th row once, then every foll 4th row, 10(12) times.
[15 sts, 51(59) shaping rows]

Left sleeve only
Work 2 rows.
Next row (WS) Cast off 2 sts, k1, p1, k1, p to last 6 sts, [K1, p1] 3 times. (13 sts)
(RS) [K1, p1] 3 times, dec right, [K1, p1] twice, k1. (11 sts)
(WS) Cast off 2 sts, k1, p to last 6 sts, [K1, p1] 3 times. (9 sts)
(RS) [K1, p1] 3 times, k1, p1, k1.
(WS) Cast off 2 sts, [K1, p1] 3 times. (7 sts)
(RS) [K1, p1] 3 times, k1.
(WS) Cast off 2 sts, [K1, p1] twice. (5 sts)
(RS) [K1, p1] twice, k1.
(WS) Cast off 2 sts, k1, p1. (3 sts)
(RS) K1, p1, k1.
Cast off rem sts.

Right sleeve only
Work 1 row.
Next row (RS) Cast off 2 sts, p1, k1, p1, k to last 6 sts, [P1, k1] 3 times. (13 sts)
(WS) [P1, k1] 3 times, p to last 4 sts, [K1, p1] twice.
(RS) Cast off 2 sts, p1, k to last 9 sts, sl 1, k2tog, psso, [P1, k1] 3 times. (9 sts)
(WS) [P1, k1] 4 times, p1.
(RS) Cast off 2 sts, [P1, k1] 3 times. (7 sts)
(WS) [P1, k1] 3 times, p1.

(RS) Cast off 2 sts, [P1, k1] twice. (5 sts)
(WS) [P1, k1] twice, p1.
(RS) Cast off 2 sts, p1, k1. (3 sts)
(WS) P1, k1, p1.
Cast off rem sts.

HOOD

Using 4.50mm (US 7) needles, cast on 150 sts.
Work in St st, beg with a k row, until length measures 12cm (4¾in), ending on a WS row.
Next row (RS) (dec) K2tog, k to last 2 sts, k2tog.
Purl 1 row.
Rep last 2 rows, 4 times more, then RS (dec) row again. St st 3 rows.
Next row(RS)(dec) K2tog, k to last 2 sts, k2tog.
Rep last 4 rows, 5 times more. [126 sts]
Purl 1 row.
Place a marker (colored thread) at center of last row.
Shape back of hood
(RS) (dec) K to within 2 sts of marker, k2tog, sl 1, k1, psso, k to end.
Purl 1 row.
Rep last 2 rows twice more.
(RS) (dec) K to within 2 sts of marker, k2tog, sl 1, k1, psso, k to end.
(WS) (dec) P to within 2 sts of marker, p2togtbl, p2tog, p to end.
Rep last 2 rows 8 times more. [84 sts, 59 shaping rows] Cast off.

MAKING UP

Press pieces gently, using a warm iron over a damp cloth.
Sew raglan sleeve seams to back and fronts. Sew sleeve seams. Sew side seams. With RS facing for Right Front, and WS facing for Left Front, rejoin yarn and cast off 10 sts on holders at front neck edges.
Attach hood Fold cast off edge in half and join for back seam, attach back seam to center back of bodice.
Sew hood into place along seams, beg and ending at front edges.
Front Bands
Using 4.00mm (US 6) needles, cast on 11 sts.
(RS) K1 * p1, k1; rep from * to end.
(WS) P1 * k1, p1; rep from * to end.
These 2 rows form rib.
Cont working in rib until length (slightly stretched) measures same as right front to beg of neck shaping, around edge of hood and down left front. Sew band into place.
Pockets (make 2)
Using 4.50mm (US 7) needles, cast on 36 sts. Cont working in St st until length measures 15cm (6in), ending on a WS row.
Sew pocket to fronts, approx 25cm (10in) above cast on edge and 6cm (2½in) from side seam.

44

36

48

54

45

44

40

50

48

52

36

A Room for Relaxing

Create a restful space where you can feel completely at ease, relaxed, and peaceful. Make a collection of scatter cushions with cables and ribs. Combine colors and textures that are soft and subtle. A felted ottoman will make a majestic statement.

Woven Knit Pillow

Cable Rib Pillow

Garter Rib Pillow

Moss Stitch Pillow

FAR LEFT

Felted Ottoman

34

Patchwork Throw

CABLE RIB PILLOW

An easy cable and rib pattern. A great project for novice cable knitters.

YARN Ella Rae CLASSIC
100g/3.5oz   200m/219yds

Col. No.	Quantity x 100g balls
10	3

MEASUREMENTS
47cm x 47cm (18½in x 18½in)

NEEDLES
1 pair 4.50mm (US 7) needles.
1 cable needle.

TENSION/GAUGE
20 sts and 24 rows measured over 10cm (4in) of St st using 4.50mm (US 7) needles. Cable Panel measures approx 5cm (2in).

ADDITIONAL REQUIREMENTS
Cushion/pillow insert:
50cm x 50cm
(19¾in x 19¾in)

SPECIAL ABBREVIATION
C8B or C8F (Cable 8 back or front)—slip next 4 sts onto cable needle and hold at back (or front) of work, knit next 4 sts from left-hand needle, then knit sts from cable needle.

CABLE PANEL (14 sts)
Row 1 P1, k12, p1.
Row 2 K1, p12, k1.
Row 3 P1, k4, C8F, p1.
Row 4 K1, p12, k1.
Row 5 & 6 As rows 1 & 2.
Row 7 P1, C8B, k4, p1.
Row 8 K1, p12, k1.0
Repeat these 8 rows.

FRONT
Using 4.50mm (US 7) needles, cast on 94 sts.
Establishment rows:
Row 1 (RS) * K3, p2, k3, p2, k3, work row 1 of cable panel;
rep from * twice more, k3, p2, k3, p2, k3.

Row 2 (WS) * P3, k2, p3, k2, p3, work row 2 of cable panel; rep from * twice more, p3, k2, p3, k2, p3.
These 2 rows set pattern.
Cont working in pattern repeat as set until length measures 47cm (18½in). Cast off.

BACK
Using 4.50mm (US 7) needles, cast on 94 sts. Work in St st for 47cm (18½in), ending on a WS row. Cast off.

MAKING UP
Using edge to edge st (or method preferred), sew along three sides. Place insert and sew rem seam. ❏

WOVEN KNIT PILLOW

A gorgeous woven effect created by a simple knit/purl combination. Suitable for a beginner knitter.

YARN Ella Rae CLASSIC
100g/3.5oz   200m/219yds

Col. No.	Quantity x 100g balls
37	3

MEASUREMENTS
50cm x 50cm
(19¾in x 19¾in)

NEEDLES
1 pair 4.50mm (US 7) needle.

TENSION/GAUGE
20 sts and 24 rows measured over 10cm (4in) of St st using 4.50mm (US 7) needles.

ADDITIONAL REQUIREMENTS
Cushion/pillow insert:
50cm x 50cm
(19¾in x 19¾in)

CUSHION (Make 2)
Using 4.50mm (US 7) needles, cast on 90 sts.
Row 1 (RS) * K18, p18; rep from * once more, k18.
Row 2 (WS) * P18, k18; rep from * once more, p18.
Repeat last 2 rows, 11 times.
Row 25 (RS) * P18, k18; rep from * once more, p18.
Row 26 (WS) * K18, p18; rep from * once more, k18.
Repeat last 2 rows, 11 times.
These 48 rows form pattern repeat.

Cont working in pattern repeat as set until length measures approx 50cm (19¾in), ending on a row 24 or 48 of pattern.
Cast off.

MAKING UP
Using edge to edge st (or method preferred), sew along three sides. Place insert and sew rem seam. ❏

PATCHWORK THROW

This beautiful throw is far simpler than it looks.

YARN Ella Rae CLASSIC		
100g/3.5oz	200m/219yds	
Col.	No.	Quantity x 100g balls
col A	13	4
col B	15	3
col C	34	1
col D	12	4
col E	28	1
col F	37	1

MEASUREMENTS
1 Square = approx 15cm x 15cm (6in x 6in)
Width 110cm (43¼in)
Length 135cm (53¼in)
NEEDLES
1 pair 4.50mm (US 7) needles.
TENSION/GAUGE
20 sts and 24 rows measured over 10cm (4in) of St st using 4.50mm (US 7) needles.
SPECIAL ABBREVIATIONS
wyrn (wrap yarn round needle)—wrap yarn around needle to make a stitch, always used before a purl st.
yf (yarn forward)—bring yarn to front to make a stitch, always used before a knit st.

SQUARE 1 (Ribbed sq.) (4 triangles form 1 square) (Make 80)
Using 4.50mm (US 7) needles and col A, cast on 27 sts.
Row 1 Purl.
Row 2 K2tog, k to last 2 sts, k2tog.
Row 3 Purl.
Change to col B.
Row 4 P2tog, p to last 2 sts, p2tog.
Row 5 Knit.
Row 6 K2tog, k to last 2 sts, k2tog.
Row 7 Purl.
Row 8 K2tog, k to last 2 sts, k2tog.
Change to col C.
Row 9 Knit.
Row 10 P2tog, p to last 2 sts, p2tog.
Row 11 Purl.
Row 12 K2tog, k to last 2 sts, k2tog.
Row 13 Purl.
Change to col D.
Row 14 P2tog, p to last 2 sts, p2tog.
Row 15 Knit.
Row 16 K2tog, k to last 2 sts, k2tog.
Row 17 Purl.
Row 18 K2tog, k to last 2 sts, k2tog.
Change to col E.
Row 19 Knit.
Row 20 P2tog, p to last 2 sts, p2tog.
Row 21 Purl.
Row 22 K2tog, k to last 2 sts, k2tog.
Row 23 Purl.
Row 24 K2tog, k1, k2tog.
Row 25 P3tog.
These 25 rows form pattern repeat.

Sew 4 triangles tog to form a square. (20 squares made)

SQUARE 2 (Plain Sq.) (Make 5 x col A, 6 x col D, 7 x col F)
Using 4.50mm (US 7) needles, cast on 27 sts.
Work in St st until length measures 15cm (6in). Cast off.

SQUARE 3 (Edge Sq.) (Make 5 x col A, 4 x col D, 5 x col F)
Using 4.50mm (US 7) needles, cast on 27 sts.
Work 4 rows st st, beg with a knit row (this becomes WS).
Next row (WS) Purl.
Cont working in St st until length measures 15cm (6in).
Cast off.

SQUARE 4 (Flower Sq.) (4 triangles form 1 square) (Make 20 x col A, 24 x col B)
Using 4.50mm (US 7) needles, beg with 1 st on needle.
Row 1 Yf, k1.
Row 2 Yf, k2.
Row 3 Wyrn, p1, yf, k1, wyrn, p1.
Row 4 Yf, k1, p3, k2.
Row 5 Wyrn, p2, [k1, yf] twice, k1, p2.
Row 6 Yf, k2, p5, k3.
Row 7 Wyrn, p3, k2, yf, k1, yf, k2, p3.
Row 8 Yf, k3, p7, k4.
Row 9 Wyrn, p4, k3, yf, k1, yf, k3, p4.
Row 10 Yf, k4, p9, k5.
Row 11 Wyrn, p5, k4, yf, k1, yf, k4, p5.

Row 12 Yf, k5, p11, k6.
Row 13 Wyrn, p6, k2togtbl, k7, k2tog, p6.
Row 14 Yf, k6, p9, k7.
Row 15 Wyrn, p7, k2togtbl, k5, k2tog, p7.
Row 16 Yf, k7, p7, k8.
Row 17 Wyrn, p8, k2togtbl, k3, k2tog, p8.
Row 18 Yf, k8, p5, k9.
Row 19 Wyrn, p9, k2togtbl, k1, k2tog, p9.
Row 20 Yf, k9, p3, k10.
Row 21 Wyrn, p10, sl 1, k2tog, psso, p10.
Row 22 Wyrn, p to end.
Row 23 Yf, k to end.
Row 24 Yf, k to end.
Row 25 Wyrn, p to end.
Cast off.
Sew 4 triangles tog to form a square. (12 squares made)

MAKING UP
Sew squares tog following diagram page 147. ❏

The colors and textures found in nature are a never ending source of inspiration.

Felted Ottoman

Moss Stitch Pillow

Garter Rib Pillow

Cable Rib Pillow

MOSS STITCH PILLOW

Moss stitch and buttoning make this simple pillow classically elegant.

YARN Ella Rae CLASSIC
100g/3.5oz 200m/219yds
Col. No. Quantity x 100g balls
15 2
MEASUREMENTS
40cm x 40cm (15¾in x 15¾in)

NEEDLES
1 pair 4.50mm (US 7) needles
TENSION/GAUGE
21 sts and 24 rows measured over
10cm (4in) of Moss st using 4.50mm
(US 7) needles.

ADDITIONAL REQUIREMENTS
Cushion/pillow insert:
40cm x 40cm
(15¾in x 15¾in)
Buttons
4 x 20mm

MOSS ST
Row 1 (RS) * K1, p1;
rep from * to end.
Rep this row throughout.

FRONT
Piece 1
Using 4.50mm (US 7) needles, cast on 75 sts.
Cont working in Moss st until length measures 17.5cm (7in), ending on a WS row, inc 3 sts. (78 sts)
Next row (RS) * K2, p2; rep from * to last 2 sts, k2.
(WS) * P2, k2; rep from * to last 2 sts, p2.
Rep last 2 rows, once more.
Buttonhole rows (RS) Rib 14 sts, cast off 2 sts, rib 14 sts, cast off 2 sts, rib 14 sts, cast off 2 sts, rib 14 sts, cast off 2 sts, rib to end.

(WS) Knit to cast off sts, turn, cast on 2 sts, turn; rep to end.
Work in rib for a further 4 rows. Cast off in rib.
Piece 2
Using 4.50mm (US 7) needles, cast on 75 sts.
Work in Moss st until length measures 22.5 cm (9in), ending on a WS row. Cast off.

BACK
Using 4.50mm (US 7) needles, cast on 75 sts. Work in Moss st until length measures 40cm (15¾in), ending on a WS row. Cast off.

MAKING UP
With WS tog, sew piece 2 of front to back, using edge to edge st (or method preferred). Sew piece 1 to back, overlapping at center. Mark position for buttons to correspond with buttonholes, sew on buttons. ❑

GARTER RIB PILLOW

This pillow is worked in a simple and easy-to-knit rib, purled on the wrong side to keep it flat.

YARN Ella Rae CLASSIC
100g/3.5oz 200m/219yds
Col. No. Quantity x 100g balls
38 2
MEASUREMENTS
40cm x 40cm
(15¾in x 15¾in)

NEEDLES
1 pair 4.50mm (US 7) needles.
TENSION/GAUGE
17 sts and 24 rows measured over
10cm (4in) of rib patt using 4.50mm
(US 7) needles.

ADDITIONAL REQUIREMENTS
Cushion/pillow insert:
40cm x 40cm
(15¾in x 15¾in)

CUSHION (Make 2)
Using 4.50mm (US 7) needles, cast on 70 sts.
Row 1 (RS) * K2, p2; rep from * to last 2 sts, k2.
Row 2 (WS) Purl.
These 2 rows set pattern.
Cont working in pattern repeat as set until length measures 40cm (15¾in), ending on a WS row. Cast off.

MAKING UP
Using edge to edge st (or method preferred), sew along three sides. Insert pillow and sew rem seam. ❑

FELTED OTTOMAN COVER

An easy project suitable for a beginner. The pieces are knitted, felted, then cut to shape and stitched together.

YARN Ella Rae CLASSIC 100g/3.5oz 200m/219yds			MEASUREMENTS	TENSION/GAUGE
Col.	No.	Quantity x 100g balls	**After Felting:**	16 sts and 26 rows measured
col A	12	2	Circumference 130cm (51¼in)	over 10cm (4in) of Moss st using
col B	06	2	Diameter 45cm (17¾in)	4.50mm (US 7) needles.
col C	08	2	Depth 20cm (8in)	ADDITIONAL
			NEEDLES	REQUIREMENTS
			1 pair 4.50mm (US 7) needles.	Foam cut to size, Elastic

Piece 1
(Make 3 in col A, 3 in col B and 3 in col C)
Using 4.50mm (US 7) needles, cast on 30 sts.
Work in St st until length measures 25cm (10in),
ending on a WS row. Cast off.

Piece 2
(Make 3 in col A, 3 in col B and 3 in col C)
Using 4.50mm (US 7) needles, cast on 30 sts.
Work in St st until length measures 20cm (8in),
ending on a WS row. Cast off.

Piece 3 (Make 1 in col A)
Using 4.50mm (US 7) needles, cast on 24 sts.
Work in St st until length measures 13cm (5in),
ending on a WS row. Cast off.

MAKING UP
Felt all pieces separately using method on page 152.
Using pattern template on page 149, enlarge
to correct size and cut out felted pieces.
Edge to edge st is used to sew all pieces tog
(or method preferred).
Note It is easier to sew cover onto foam as
you go as it needs to be stretched and fit firmly.
Lay top pieces in correct position to correspond with
side pieces and sew tog. Sew center piece.
Sew elastic around edge of cover base to hold
cover in place.
Sew side pieces tog (piece 1), alternating colors. ❏

Looking out from my studio across the bay I see Breaksea Island. The purple grays of the granite lighthouse set against the deep blue sea have inspired the palette of colors for this patchwork throw.

Checkered Throw

CHECKERED THROW

This simple throw is a timeless classic, knitted in pieces then sewn together with a simple cross stitch for added effect.

YARN Ella Rae CLASSIC HEATHERS
100g/3.5oz 200m/219yds

Col.	No.	Quantity x 100g balls
col A	101	3
col B	102	3
col C	127	3
col D	103	1

MEASUREMENTS
Width approx 100cm (39½in)
Length approx 150cm (59in)
NEEDLES
1 pair 4.50mm (US 7) needles.
TENSION/GAUGE
20 sts and 24 rows measured over 10cm of St st using 4.50mm (US 7) needles.

THROW

Squares

Using 4.50mm (US 7) needles, cast on 40 sts.
Work 20cm (8in) in St st, ending on a WS row.
Cast off.

Make 13 squares each in col's A and B.
Make 14 squares in col C.

Press squares using a warm iron over a damp cloth.
Lay squares out and place together in following order:
Row 1 Col C, col B, col A, col C, col B.

Row 2 Col A, col C, col B, col A, col C.
Row 3 Col B, col A, col C, col B, col A.
Row 4 As row 1.
Row 5 As row 2.
Row 6 As row 3.
Row 7 As row 1.
Row 8 As row 2.

Sew squares together using edge to edge st.
Using col D, cross st along all seams, using photo as a guide. ❏

DOUBLE RIB THROW

Another project showing that simplicity can have maximum effect.

YARN Ella Rae CLASSIC SUPERWASH
100g/3.5oz 200m/219yds

Col.	No.	Quantity x 100g balls
32		10

MEASUREMENTS
Width approx 110cm (43¼in)
Length approx 150cm (59in)

NEEDLES
1 pair 4.50mm (US 7) needles.
1 set 4.50mm (US 7) circular needles.
TENSION/GAUGE
20 sts and 24 rows measured over 10cm (4in) of St st using 4.50mm (US 7) needles.

NOTE A circular needle is used to hold the large number of sts. Throw is worked in rows, not rounds.

Pattern Repeat (Multiple 19+8)
(RS) * K9, [p1,k1] 5 times; rep from * 9 times more, k8.
(WS) * P9, [K1B,p1] 5 times; rep from * 9 times more, p8.
These 2 rows form pattern repeat.

THROW

Using 4.50mm (US 7) circular needles, cast on 198 sts.
Cont working in pattern repeat until length measures approx 148cm (58¼in), ending on a WS row.
Cast off.

Press using a warm iron over a damp cloth.

Ribbed Edging

Using 4.50mm (US 7) needles, cast on 11 sts.
Row 1 (RS) * P1, k1; rep from * to last st, p1.
Row 2 (WS) K1, * sl 1 wyif, k1; rep from * to end.
These 2 rows form rib.
Cont working in rib until length measures same as width of throw, ending on a WS row. Cast off.
Sew rib to cast on edge of throw.
Repeat for cast off edge.
Make 2 more lengths long enough to fit along rem edges of throw. Sew into place. ❏

Both these throws are suitable for a beginner knitter.

Double Rib Throw

PINWHEEL CUSHION

A quick project for beginner knitters, these cushions are sure to impress.

YARN Ella Rae CLASSIC SUPERWASH		
100g/3.5oz 200m/219yds		
Col.	No.	Quantity x 100g balls
Version 1		
col A	22	2
col B	25	1
col C	12	1
col D	36	1
Version 2		
col A	36	2
col B	12	1
col C	25	1
col D	22	1

MEASUREMENTS
Diameter 35cm (13¾n)

NEEDLES
1 pair 4.50mm (US 7) needles.

TENSION/GAUGE
20 sts and 24 rows measured over 10cm (4in)
of St st using 4.50mm (US 7) needles.

ADDITIONAL REQUIREMENTS
40cm (15¾in) round cushion insert
2 large buttons

CUSHION

BACK
Using col A, cast on 14 sts.
Row 1 (RS) K1, * k into front and back of next st; rep from * to last st, k1. (26 sts)
Row 2 (WS) (and all alt rows) Purl.
Row 3 K2, * m1, k2; rep from * to end. (38 sts)
Row 5 K1, * m1, k3; rep from * to last st, k1. (50 sts)
Row 7 As row 5. (66 sts)
Row 9 K1, * m1, k4; rep from * to last st, k1. (82 sts)
Work 3 rows in St st.
Row 13 (RS) K1, * m1, k5; rep from * to last st, k1. (98 sts)
Work 3 rows in St st.
Row 17 (RS) K1, * m1, k6; rep from * to last st, k1. (114 sts)
Cont to inc on every foll 4th row, adding an extra st after each m1 as before, until there are 12 sts after each m1.
(210 sts, 44 rows)
Work 3 rows St st.
Cast off.

FRONT
Work as for back in color sequence as foll:
Using col D, cast on 14 sts.
* 2 rows col D.
4 rows col C.
2 rows col D.
2 rows col A.
2 rows col B.
4 rows col C.
2 rows col A.
4 rows col B. **

Work from * to ** once more. (44 rows)
3 rows col D.
Cast off.

MAKING UP
Press pieces gently, using a warm iron over a damp cloth.
With WS tog, sew front and back pieces together using edge to edge st (or method preferred), leaving an opening big enough to fit cushion insert through.
Insert cushion and sew rem of seam.
Sew button to center of cushion. ❏

CABLE & GARTER STITCH THROW

A challenging project, this throw is worked with 2 different cable panels and garter stitch columns.

YARN Ella Rae CLASSIC SUPERWASH
100g/3.5oz   200m/219yds

Col. No.	Quantity x 100g balls
25	14

MEASUREMENTS
Width approx 100cm (39½in)
Length approx 150cm (59in)

NEEDLES
1 set 4.50mm (US 7) circular needles.
1 cable needle.

TENSION/GAUGE
20 sts and 24 rows measured over 10cm (4in) St st using 4.50mm (US 7) needles.

SPECIAL ABBREVIATIONS
C4B or C4F (Cable 4 Back or Cable 4 Front) = slip next 2 sts onto cable needle and hold at back (or front) of work, knit next 2 sts from left-hand needle, then knit sts from cable needle.
C6B or C6F (Cable 6 Back or Cable 6 Front) = slip next 3 sts onto cable needle and hold at back (or front) of work, knit next 3 sts from left-hand needle, then knit sts from cable needle.
NOTE A circular needle is used to hold the large number of sts. Throw is worked in rows, not rounds.

Cable Panel A (12 sts)
Rows 1,3,5,9,11+13 (RS) P1, k4, p2, k4, p1.
Row 2 (and all foll alt rows) Work each st as it presents.
Row 7 * P1, C4F, p1; rep from * once more.
Row 15 * P1, C4B, p1; rep from * once more.
Row 16 As row 2.
Repeat these 16 rows throughout.

Cable Panel B (9 sts)
Rows 1,5,7,11,15+17 (RS) K9.
Row 2 (and all foll alt rows) Work each st as it presents.
Rows 3+9 K3, C6F.
Rows 13+19 C6B, k3.
Row 20 As row 2.
Repeat these 20 rows throughout.

THROW
Using 4.50mm circular needles, cast on 267 sts.

Establishment rows
(RS) * K5, work row 1 Cable Panel B, k5, work row 1 Cable Panel A ** ;
repeat from * to ** 7 times more, k5, work row 1 Cable Panel B, k5.
(WS) * K5, work row 2 Cable Panel B, k5, work row 2 Cable Panel A ** ; repeat from * to ** 7 times more, k5, work row 2 Cable Panel B, k5.
These 2 rows set the pattern.

Cont working in pattern as set until length measures approx 147cm (58in), ending on a WS row. Cast off.

Press using a warm iron over a damp cloth.

Ribbed Edging
Using 4.50mm (US 7) needles, cast on 11 sts.
Row 1 (RS) * P1, k1; rep from * to last st, p1.
Row 2 (WS) K1, * sl 1 wyif, k1; rep from * to end.
These 2 rows form rib.
Cont working in rib until length measures approx 100cm (39½in), ending on a WS row. Cast off.

Sew rib to cast on edge of throw, stretching or easing slightly to fit. Repeat for cast off edge. Make 2 more lengths long enough to fit along rem edges of throw. Sew into place. ❏

FELTED TOTE

A felting project for the more adventurous knitter.

YARN Ella Rae CLASSIC
100g/3.5oz 200m/219yds

Col.	No.	Quantity x 100g balls
col A	17	2
col B	29	1
col C	35	1

NEEDLES
1 pair 4.50mm (US 7) needles.

TENSION/GAUGE
20 sts and 24 rows measured over 10cm (4in) of St st using 4.50mm (US 7) needles.

MEASUREMENTS
Before felting:
Top approx 55cm (21½in)
Base approx 45cm (17¾in)
Depth approx 32cm (12½in)
After felting:
Top approx 50cm (19½in)
Base approx 40cm (15¾in)
Depth approx 25cm (10in)
ADDITIONAL REQUIREMENTS
1 Button

SPECIAL ABBREVIATIONS
LT (Left Twist). With right-hand needle behind left-hand needle, skip one st and knit the second st in back loop; then insert right-hand needle into the backs of both sts (the skipped st and the second st) and k2togtbl.

Bonbon Pattern

Row 1 (WS) Col A Knit.
Row 2 Col B K6, * sl 2 wyib, k8; rep to end, sl 2, k6.
Row 3 Col B P4, * sl 6 wyif, p4; rep from * to end.
Row 4 Col B K4, * sl 6 wyib, k4; rep from * to end.
Row 5 Col B P6, * sl 2 wyif, p8; rep from * to end.
Row 6 Col A K6, * LT, k8; rep from * to end LT, k6.
Row 7 Col A Knit.
Row 8 Col C K1, * sl 2 wyib, k8; rep from * to end sl 2, k1.
Row 9 Col C P1, sl 4 wyif, * p4, sl 6 wyif; rep from * to end p4, sl 4, p1.
Row 10 Col C K1, sl 4 wyib, * k4, sl 6 wyib; rep from * to end k4, sl 4, k1.
Row 11 Col C P1, * sl 2 wyif, p8; rep from * to end sl 2, p1.
Row 12 Col A K1, * LT, k8; rep from * to end LT, k1.
These 12 rows form pattern repeat.

Note: Piece is worked from top to bottom.

FRONT and BACK (make 2)

Using 4.50mm (US 7) needles and col A, cast on 114 sts.
Knit 4 rows.
Now cont working in pattern repeat.
Keeping pattern correct, dec 1 st each end next row then 1 st each end every foll 12th row, 7 times. (100 sts)
Cont working in pattern until length measures approx 30cm (11¾in), ending on either a row 1 or 7 of pattern repeat. Cast off.

BASE

Using 4.50mm (US 7) needles and col A, cast on 22 sts.
Working in St st, inc 1 st each end every alt row, 5 times. (32 sts)
Cont working in St st until length measures 40cm (15¾in), ending on a WS row.
Dec 1 st each end next row, then 1 st each end foll alt rows, 4 times. (22 sts)
Purl 1 row. Cast off.

HANDLES (make 2)

Using 4.50mm (US 7) needles and col A, cast on 14 sts.
Work in St st for 56cm, (22in) ending on a WS row.
Cast off. Sew seam lengthwise.

FASTENER

Using 4.50mm (US 7) needles and col A, cast on 18 sts.
Work in St st for 8cm (3¾in), ending on a WS row.
Buttonhole row (RS): K8 sts, cast off 3 sts, k to end.
(WS) P to cast off sts, turn, cast on 3 sts, turn, p to end.
(RS) Dec 1 st each end every row until 6 sts rem. Cast off.

MAKING UP

Felt all pieces separately (see method pg 152).
Sew side seams of front and back tog.
Sew base to front and back.
Sew handles approx 7cm (3in) in from side edge.
Sew fastener to center of back.
Sew button to front. ❏

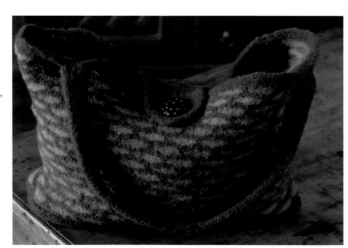

60

62

72

64

62

66

65

74

70

A Room for Sharing

The kitchen is the heart of the home, the perfect place for sharing. Sharing plans for the day ahead, sharing a meal with family and friends, sharing stories and laughter . . .
Sharing enriches our lives.

Sunday brunch with family and friends,
tea with toast and marmalade . . .
these are a few of my favorite things.

TEA COZY

A unique breakfast set to knit.

YARN Ella Rae CLASSIC
100g/3.5oz 200m/219yds

Col. No.	Quantity x 100g balls
59	1

MEASUREMENTS
Circumference 48cm (19in)
Height 24cm (9½in)

NEEDLES
1 pair 4.00mm (US 6) needles.
1 pair 4.50mm (US 7) needles.

TENSION/GAUGE
21 sts and 24 rows measured over 10cm (4in) of Moss st using 4.50mm (US 7) needles.

MOSS ST

(RS) K1 * p1, k1; rep from * to end.
(WS) Rep RS row.
These 2 rows form pattern repeat.

MOSS RIB

Row 1 (RS) * K2, p3, k1; rep from * to last st, k1.
(WS) P1 * k1, p1, k1, p1, k1, p1; rep from * to end.
These 2 rows form pattern repeat.

PATTERN

Front and Back

Using 4.00mm (US 6) needles, cast on 49 sts.
Cont working in Moss st until length measures 3cm (1¼in), ending on a WS row.
Change to 4.50mm (US 7) needles.
Cont working in Moss rib until length measures 10cm (4in), ending on a WS row.
Cont working in Moss st until length measures 18cm (7in), ending on a RS row.
(WS) Knit.
(RS) * K2, yf, k2tog; rep from * to last st, k1.
(WS) Knit.
Work 2 rows in Moss st.
(RS) * K into front, back and front of each st; rep from * to end. (147 sts)
(WS) Knit.
(RS) Cast off.

MAKING UP

Sew front and back pieces tog using edge to edge st (or preferred method), leaving an opening for the spout and handle.
Using 6 strands of yarn, braid a length of cord and thread through eyelets. ❏

Breakfast Set

EGG COZY AND CUP WARMERS

Delicate ruffles add charm to this breakfast set.

YARN Ella Rae CLASSIC
100g/3.5oz   200m/219yds

Col. No.   Quantity x 100g balls
59   1

MEASUREMENTS
Cup Warmer
Circumference 24cm (9½in)
Height 10cm (4in)
Egg Cozy
Circumference 15cm (6in)
Height 8cm (3¼in)

NEEDLES
1 pair 4.50mm (US 7) needles.
TENSION/GAUGE—Egg Cozy
20 sts and 24 rows measured over 10cm (4in)
of St st using 4.50mm (US 7) needles.
TENSION/GAUGE—Cup Warmer
21 sts and 24 rows measured over 10cm (4in)
of Moss st using 4.50mm (US 7) needles.
ADDITIONAL REQUIREMENTS
2 small shell buttons.

EGG COZY

Base

Using 4.50mm (US 7) needles, cast on 18 sts.
Cont working in St st until length measures 5cm (2in),
ending on a WS row.
Next row (RS) (dec) Dec 1 st each end next row,
then 1 st each end every foll row 3 times more. (10 sts)
Cast off rem sts.

Sew seams.

Ruffles

Using 4.50mm (US 7) needles, cast on 340 sts.
Row 1 * K2, pass 2nd st over first st; rep from * to end. (170 sts)
Row 2 * P2tog; rep from * to end. (85 sts)
Cast off rem sts.

Sew ruffle to base, beginning at cast on edge and side
seam of base.
Slowly wind the ruffle around and up toward top
(cast off edge) of base, stitching into place as you go. ❏

Handy Tip

To fix a dropped stitch, *use a crochet hook to knit or
purl each stitch up the ladder until you reach the row
being worked. Always purl the purl stitches and knit the
knit stitches to keep the pattern correct.*

CUP WARMERS

Moss st

(RS) K1 * p1, k1; rep from * to end.
(WS) Rep RS row.
These 2 rows form pattern repeat.

Pattern

Using 4.50mm (US 7) needles, cast on 156 sts.
Row 1 (RS) * K2, pass 2nd st over first st;
rep from * to end.
Row 2 * P2tog; rep from * to end. (39 sts)
Cont working in Moss st until length
measures 3cm (1¼in), ending on a WS row.
Buttonhole row (RS) P1, k1, yf, k2tog,
patt to end.
Work a further 1cm (½in) in Moss st,
ending on a WS row.
Rep buttonhole row.
Cont working in Moss st for a further 3cm (1¼in),
ending on a WS row.
(RS) * K into front and back of each st;
rep from * to end. (78 sts)
(WS) P into back and front of every st. (156 sts)
Knit 1 row.
(WS) Cast off k/wise.

Sew buttons to correspond with buttonholes. ❏

RIBBED FINGERLESS GLOVES

These handy little arm-warmers are easy to knit and great for wintery mornings.

YARN Ella Rae AMITY
100g/3.5oz   182m/200yds

Col. No.	Quantity x 100g balls
23	1

MEASUREMENTS
To fit an average adult.

NEEDLES
1 pair 5.00mm (US 8) needles.

TENSION/GAUGE
20 sts and 24 rows measured over 10cm (4in) of St st using 5.00mm (US 8) needles.

RIGHT GLOVE

Using 5.00mm needles, cast on 32 sts.
Work 20cm (8in) in k2, p2 rib, ending on a WS row. **
(RS) Rib 16, inc 1 st, k1, inc 1 st, rib to end. (34 sts)
Work 3 rows.
(RS) Rib 16, inc 1 st, rib 3 sts, inc 1 st, rib to end. (36 sts)
Work 3 rows.
(RS) Rib 16, inc 1 st, rib 5 sts, inc 1 st, rib to end. (38 sts)
Work 3 rows.
(RS) Rib 16, inc 1 st, rib 7 sts, inc 1 st, rib to end. (40 sts)
Work 3 rows.
(RS) Rib 16, inc 1 st, rib 9 sts, inc 1 st, rib to end. (42 sts)
Work 3 rows.

Thumb
(RS) Rib 29 sts, turn.

(WS) Rib 10 sts, turn, cast on 2 sts.
Work 7 rows in rib on these 12 sts. Cast off.
With RS facing, rejoin yarn and pickup 2 sts from cast on sts at base of thumb, rib to end. (34 sts)
Work a further 5cm (2in), ending on a WS row. Cast off in rib.

LEFT GLOVE

Work as for right glove to **.
(RS) Rib 13, inc 1 st, p1, inc 1 st, rib to end. (34 sts)
Work 3 rows.
(RS) Rib 13, inc 1 st, rib 3 sts, inc 1 st, rib to end. (36 sts)
Work 3 rows.
(RS) Rib 13, inc 1 st, rib 5 sts, inc 1 st, rib to end. (38 sts)
Work 3 rows.
(RS) Rib 13, inc 1 st, rib 7 sts, inc 1 st, rib to end. (40 sts)
Work 3 rows.
(RS) Rib 13, inc 1 sts, rib 9 sts, inc 1 st, rib to end. (42 sts)
Work 3 rows.

Thumb
(RS) Rib 29 sts, turn, cast on 2 sts.
(WS) Rib 10 sts, turn.
Work 7 rows in rib on these 12 sts. Cast off.
With WS facing, pickup 2 sts from cast on sts at base of thumb, rib to end. (34 sts)
Work a further 5cm (2in), ending on a WS row. Cast off in rib.

MAKING UP

Press pieces gently using a warm iron over a damp cloth.
Join thumb seam and side seam. ❏

PLACE MATS

Worked in durable Tweed stitch, these place mats are stylish and practical.

YARN Ella Rae CLASSIC SUPERWASH			NEEDLES
100g/3.5oz 200m/219yds			1 pair 4.00mm (US 6) needles.
Col. No.		Quantity x 100g balls	TENSION/GAUGE
col A 18 taupe		1	23.5 sts and 38 rows measured over
col B 23 steele grey		1	10cm (4 in) of Tweed st using 4.00mm
MEASUREMENTS			(US 6) needles.
Width approx 25cm (10in)			
Length approx 35cm (13¾in)			

Tweed Stitch

Row 1 (RS) K1 * yf, sl 1 p/wise, yb, k1;
rep from * to end.
Row 2 K1, p1 * yb, sl p/wise, yf, p1;
rep from * to last st, k1.
These 2 rows form patt rep.

PLACE MATS

Using col A, cast on 65 sts.
Work 3cm (1¼in) in patt rep,
ending on a WS row.
* Change to col B.
Work 2 rows of pattern.
Change to col A.
Work 2 rows of pattern. **
Cont working from * to ** until length
measures 32cm (12½in), ending
with a col B and WS row.
Cont working in col A and patt rep
until length measures 35cm (13¾in),
ending on a WS row. Cast off. ❏

CASUAL ROLL-NECK SWEATER

Throw this on over a T-shirt for casual wear. A great beginner knit.

YARN Ella Rae CLASSIC				
100g/3.5oz 200m/219yds				
	A	B	C	D
Bust	81	86	91	97 cm
Col. No.	Quantity x 100g balls			
13	4	4	5	5
MEASUREMENTS				
Refer to diagram on page 148.				

NEEDLES
1 pair 4.00mm (US 6) needles.
1 pair 4.50mm (US 7) needles.
1 4.00mm (US 6) circular needle.
TENSION/GAUGE
20 sts and 24 rows measured over 10cm (4in) of St st using 4.50mm (US 7) needles.

FRONT

Using 4.00mm (US 6) needles, cast on 90(96,108,120) sts.
Work in k3, p3 rib for 6cm (2¼in), ending on a WS row.
Change to 4.50mm (US 7) needles.
Cont working in St st until length (incl band) measures 26(24,26,24)cm, [10¼(9½,10¼,9½) in], ending on a WS row.
Shape sides (RS) Inc 1 st each end next row, then 1 st each end foll 6th rows, 3 times, then on foll 4th rows, once.
[100(106,118,130) sts, 23 shaping rows]
Place a marker. **
Cont working straight until length (incl band) measures 47(47,49,49)cm, [18½(18½,19¼,19¼) in], ending on a WS row.
Shape front neck (RS) K43(46,52,58)sts, turn, leave rem sts on a holder.
(WS) Cast off 2(2,4,4) sts at beg (neck edge) next row.
Knit 1 row.
(WS) Dec 1 st at neck edge next row, then at neck edge every foll row, 10 times. [30(33,37,43) sts]
St st 4 rows.
Cast off rem sts.
With RS facing, leave 14 center sts on a holder.
Rejoin yarn to rem sts.
(RS) Cast off 2(2,4,4) sts, knit to end.
Purl 1 row.
(RS) Dec 1 st at neck edge next row, then at neck edge every foll row, 10 times. [30(33,37,43) sts]
St st 3 rows. Cast off rem sts.

BACK

Work as for front to **.
Cont working straight until length (incl band) measures 52(52,54,54)cm, [20½(20½,21¼,21¼ in], ending on a WS row.
Shape back neck (RS) K43(46,52,58) sts, turn, leave rem sts on a holder.

(WS) Cast off 7(7,8,8) sts, purl to end.
(RS) Knit.
(WS) Cast off 6(6,7,7) sts, purl to end.
Cast off rem 30(33,37,43) sts.
With RS facing, leave 14 center sts on holder.
Rejoin yarn to rem sts.
(RS) Cast off 7(7,8,8) sts, knit to end.
(WS) Purl.
(RS) Cast off 6(6,7,7) sts, knit to end.
(WS) Purl.
Cast off rem 30(33,37,43) sts.

MAKING UP

Press pieces gently on WS, using a warm iron over a damp cloth. Join shoulder seams.
Neckband With RS facing, using 4.00mm (US 6) circular needle, beg at right shoulder seam, pickup and knit 7(7,8,8) sts along back neck, 14 sts from holder, 7(7,8,8) sts along rem side of back neck, 13(13,14,14) sts down left side front neck, 14 sts from holder, 13(13,14,14) sts along right side front neck. [68(68,72,72) sts]
Work in k2, p2 rib until length measures 18cm (7in), ending on a WS row. Cast off loosely in rib.
Armbands Using 4.00mm (US 6) needles, pickup and knit 56(56,56,60) sts along armhole edge between markers.
Work in k2, p2 rib for 4cm (1½in), ending on a WS row.
Cast off loosely in rib. Join side seams and band seams. ❑

Handy Tip

When you finish knitting for the day, always finish at the end of a row. If you stop in the middle and then leave your work for a length of time, you may find that when you resume knitting the fabric is uneven. Avoid this by completing a full row.

The kitchen table is the best place to share your thoughts and plan the day. Take time to share a leisurely breakfast with your family.

My grandmother Winnifred Ann's tea set inspired this tea cozy. Every Thursday I enjoy afternoon tea with my mom, and there's nothing better than tea in fine china.

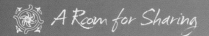

WINNIFRED ANN TEA COZY

A challenging project using fairisle and garter stitch.

YARN Ella Rae CLASSIC		
100g/3.5oz 200m/219yds		
Col.	No.	Quantity x 100g balls
col A	39	1
col B	35	1
col C	38	1
col D	14	1
col E	23	1

MEASUREMENTS
Width (at base) 30cm (11¾in)
Height 22cm (8½in)
NEEDLES
1 pair 4.50mm (US 7) needles.
TENSION/GAUGE
20 sts and 24 rows measured over
10cm (4in) of St st using 4.50mm
(US 7) needles.

SPECIAL ABBREVIATIONS
ch 4 (chain 4 sts) knit next st,
* place st back onto left-hand
needle and knit again; rep from *
twice more.

Using 4.50mm (US 7) needles and col A, cast on 68 sts.
Rows 1–3 col A knit.
Rows 4 Col B knit.
Rows 5 Col B k2, * col C ch 4, col B k2; rep from * to end.
Rows 6 Col B knit.
Rows 7–11 Col A knit.
Rows 12 * Col D k2, col A k3; rep from * to last st, k1.
Rows 13 Col A knit.
Rows 14 As row 12.
Rows 15–16 Col A knit.
Row 17 Col A knit.
Row 18 Col C knit.
Rows 19–21 Col A knit.
Row 22 * Col E k2, col A k3; rep from * to end.
Row 23 Col E knit.
Row 24 * Col E k2, col D k3; rep from * to end.
Row 25 As row 23.
Row 26 As row 24.
Row 27+28 Col D knit.
Row 29 * Col A k1, col D k1; rep from * to end.
Row 30+31 Col D knit.
Row 32 * Col E k2, col D k3; rep from * to end.
Row 33 Col B knit.
Row 34 * Col E k2, col B k3; rep from * to end.
Row 35 As row 33.
Row 36 As row 34.
Rows 37+38 As row 33.

Row 39 * Col B k1, col C k1; rep from * to end.
Row 40 As row 33.
Row 41 Col B k2tog, knit to last 2 sts, k2tog.
Row 42 Col B p2tog, p to last 2 sts, p2tog.
Row 43 Col B k2tog, k3, *col C k1, col B k3; rep from * to last 2 sts, k2tog.
Row 44 As row 42.
Row 45 Col B k4, * col C k1, col B k3; rep from * to end.
Row 46 As row 42.
Row 47 Col B k1, * col C k1, col B k3; rep from * to end.
Row 48 As row 42.
Row 49 * Col B k1, col A k1; rep from * to end.
Row 50 Col E k2tog, k to last 2 sts, k2tog.
Row 51 Col E k2, * col D ch 4, col E k2; rep from * to last 3 sts, k3.
Row 52 As row 50.
Row 53 Col B knit.
Row 54 Col B p2tog, p to last 2 sts, p2tog.
Row 55 Col B cast off 2 sts, k2, * col C k1, col B k3; rep from * to last 4 sts, k4.
Row 56 Col B cast off 2 sts, p to end.
Repeat last 2 rows 6 times more.
Cast off rem sts.

MAKING UP
Darn in all ends on WS.
With RS tog, sew pieces tog using backstitch.
Make a cord using 3 strands each of col's A and C.
Twist or braid strands tog and sew along seam. ❏

CABLE SOCKS

These chunky cable socks are great for around the house or wearing under boots.

YARN Ella Rae CLASSIC HEATHERS
100g/3.5oz 200m/219yds

Col. No. Quantity x 100g balls
137 2

MEASUREMENTS
To fit an average adult, length can be adjusted.

NEEDLES
1 set 4.50mm (US 7) double ended needles.

TENSION/GAUGE
20 sts and 24 rows measured over 10cm (4in) of St st using 4.50mm (US 7) needles.

SPECIAL ABBREVIATIONS

C4F or C4B (Cable 4 Front or Cable 4 Back) slip next 2 sts onto cable needle and hold at front (or back) of work, knit next 2 sts from left-hand needle, then knit sts from cable needle.
C3B (Cable 3 Back) slip next st onto cable needle and hold at back of work, knit next 2 sts from left-hand needle, then knit st from cable needle.
C3F (Cable 3 Front) slip next 2 sts onto cable needle and hold at front of work, knit next st from left-hand needle then knit sts from cable needle.
T3B (Twist 3 Back) slip next st onto cable needle and hold at back of work, knit next 2 sts from left-hand needle then purl st from cable needle.
T3F (Twist 3 Front) slip next 2 sts onto cable needle and hold at front of work, purl next st from left-hand needle then knit sts from cable needle.

SOCKS

Loosely cast on 52 sts. Divide sts onto 3 needles. (18-16-18)

Round 1 * K2tbl, p2; rep from * to end.

Rep this round for 6cm (2½in).

Next rnd Rnd 1 P1, k2, p2, k8, p2, k2, p1, k2, p2, k8, p2, k2, p1, k2, p2, k8, p2, k2, p1.

Rnd 2 As rnd 1.

Rnd 3 P1, k2, p3, C3B, T3F, p3, k2, p1, k2, p3, C3B, T3F, p3, k2, p1, k2, p3, C3B, T3F, p3, k2, p1.

Rnd 4 P1, k2, p3, k3, p1, k2, p3, k3, p1, k2, p3, k3, p1, k2, p3, k2, p1, k2, p3, k3, p1, k2, p3, k2, p1.

Rnd 5 P1, k2, p2, T3B, k1, p1, C3F, p2, k2, p1, k2, p2, T3B, k1, p1, C3F, p2, k2, p1, k2, p2, T3B, k1, p1, C3F, p2, k2, p1.

Rnd 6 P1, k2, p2, k2, p1, k1, p1, k3, p2, k2, p1, k2, p2, k2, p1, k1, p1, k3, p2, k2, p1, k2, p2, k2, p1, k1, p1, k3, p2, k2, p1.

Rnd 7 P1, k2, p1, C3B, [p1,k1] twice, T3F, p1, k2, p1, k2, p1, C3B, [p1,k1] twice, T3F, p1, k2, p1, k2, p1, C3B, [p1,k1] twice, T3F, p1, k2, p1.

Rnd 8 P1, k2, p1, k3, p1, [k1,p1] twice, k2, p1, k2, p1, k2, p1, k3, p1, [k1,p1] twice, k2, p1, k2, p1, k2, p1, k3, p1, [k1,p1] twice, k2, p1, k2, p1.

Rnd 9 P1, k2, T3B, [k1,p1] 3 times, C3F, k2, p1, k2, T3B, [k1,p1] 3 times, C3F, k2, p1, k2, T3B, [k1,p1] 3 times, C3F, k2, p1.

Rnd 10 P1, k4, p1, [k1,p1] 3 times, k5, p1, k4, p1, [k1,p1] 3 times, k5, p1, k4, p1, [k1,p1] 3 times, k5, p1.

Rnd 11 P1, k2, T3F, [k1,p1] 3 times, T3B, k2, p1, k2, T3F, [k1,p1] 3 times, T3B, k2, p1, k2, T3F, [k1,p1] 3 times, T3B, k2, p1.

Rnd 12 As rnd 8.

Rnd 13 P1, k2, p1, T3F, [p1,k1] twice, T3B, p1, k2, p1, k2, p1, T3F, [p1,k1] twice, T3B, p1,k2, p1, k2, p1, T3F, [p1,k1] twice, T3B, p1, k2, p1.

Rnd 14 As rnd 6.

Rnd 15 P1, k2, p2, T3F, k1, p1, T3B, p2, k2, p1, k2, p2, T3F, k1, p1, T3B, p2, k2, p1, k2, p2, T3F, k1, p1, T3B, p2, k2, p1.

Rnd 16 As rnd 4.

Rnd 17 P1, k2, p3, T3F, T3B, p3, k2, p1, k2, p3, T3F, T3B, p3, k2, p1, k2, p3, T3F, T3B, p3, k2, p1.

Rnd 18 P1, k2, p4, k4, p4, k2, p1, k2, p4, k4, p4, k2, p1, k2, p4, k4, p4, k2, p1.

Rnd 19 P1, k2, p2, C4B, C4F, p2, k2, p1, k2, p2, C4B, C4F, p2, k2, p1, k2, p2, C4B, C4F, p2, k2, p1.

Rnd 20 P1, k2, p2, k8, p2, k2, p1, k2, p2, k8, p2, k2, p1, k2, p2, k8, p2, k2, p1.

Rnds 21+22 As rnds 1+2.

Rnds 23+24 As rnds 19+20.

These 24 rounds set the cable pattern.

Work 42 rounds more in cable pattern. (Total of 66 rounds worked)

(Heel) Knit the first 13 sts of rnd onto 1 needle, slip the last 13 sts of rnd onto other end of same needle (these 26 sts are for heel).

Leave rem sts on 2 needles for instep.

Working on the 26 sts for heel.

Knit 21 rows in St st.

To turn heel K17, k2tog, k1, turn.

P12, p2tog, p1, turn.

K13, k2tog, k1, turn.

P14, p2tog, p1, turn.

K15, k2tog, k1, turn.

Cont working as set until all sts are on 1 needle. (19 sts)

Next row P2tog, p to last 2 sts, p2tog. (17 sts)

Knit back 8 sts (heel is complete).

Slip all instep sts onto one needle. Using another needle knit rem 8 sts of heel then knit up 14 sts along side of heel.

With a second needle, patt across instep sts (cont to work cable pattern as it presents instep sts only). Using a third needle knit up 14 sts along other side of heel then rem 9 sts. (71 sts)

Dec for instep as foll:

Rnd 1 Knit.

Rnd 2 1st needle; knit to last 4 sts, k2tog, k2.

2nd needle; patt. **3rd needle;** k2, sl 1, k1, psso, k to end. Rep last 2 rnds until 13 sts rem on 1st and 3rd needles. Cont without shaping until foot measures 15cm (6in) (or length desired) from the side of heel where sts were knitted up. (To end the cable pattern after a diamond at the toe, we worked to rnd 18 of cable pattern).

Shape toe

Rnd 1 1st needle; knit to last last 3 sts, k2tog, k1.

2nd needle; k1, sl 1, k1, psso, knit to last 3 sts, k2tog, k1.

3rd needle; k1, sl 1, k1, psso, knit to end. Rep this rnd until 13 sts rem.

Work 1 rnd without shaping then 1st needle of next rnd. Slip sts on 3rd needle onto end of 1st needle then sts tog. Press lightly using a warm iron over a damp cloth. ❏

FINGERLESS MITTENS

You can never have too many of these practical little mittens.

YARN Ella Rae CLASSIC HEATHERS
100g/3.5oz 200m/219yds

Col. No. Quantity x 100g balls
118   1

MEASUREMENTS
Adult size, length - 30cm (11¾in)

NEEDLES
1 pair 4.00mm (US 6) needles.
1 pair 4.50mm (US 7) needles.

TENSION/GAUGE
20 sts and 24 rows measured over 10cm
(4in)of St st using 4.50mm (US 7) needles.

RIGHT GLOVE

Using 4.00mm (US 6) needles, cast on 32 sts.

Work 10 rows in St st.

Change to 4.50mm (US 7) needles. Cont working in St st until length measures 17cm (6¾in), ending on a WS row. **

(RS) K16, inc 1 st, k1, inc 1 st, k13. (34 sts)

St st 3 rows.

(RS) K16, inc 1 st, k3, inc 1 st, k13. (36 sts)

St st 3 rows.

(RS) K16, inc 1 st, k5, inc 1 st, k13. (38 sts)

Cont to inc 2 sts every 4th row as set until there are 42 sts.

St st 3 rows.

Thumb

Next row (RS) K29 sts, turn.

(WS) K1, p9, turn, cast on 3 sts.

*** Work 11 rows on these 13 sts.

Cast off.

With RS facing, rejoin yarn and pickup and knit 3 sts from cast on sts at base of thumb, k to end. (35 sts)

Work a further 5cm (2in) in St st, ending on a WS row.

Cast off.

LEFT GLOVE

Work as for right glove to **.

Next row (RS) K13, inc 1 st, k1, inc 1 st, k16. (34 sts)

St st 3 rows.

(RS) K13, inc 1 st, k3, inc 1 st, k16. (36 sts)

Cont to inc 2 sts every 4th row as set, until there are 42 sts.

St st 3 rows.

Thumb

Next row (RS) K29 sts, turn, cast on 3 sts.

(WS) K1, p12, turn.

Work as for right glove from *** to end.

MAKING UP

Press pieces gently using a warm iron over a damp cloth.

Join thumb seam and side seam. ❑

These fingerless mittens are so easy to knit, you will want a pair in every color.

81

80

86

90

84

92

92

88

A Room for Retreating

Here is where we enjoy spending time without distraction, reading a novel, catching up on that classic movie, resting, and recharging—where we surround ourselves with personal trinkets and things that hold special memories close to our hearts—the space we retreat to when we need time out.

At the end of a busy day there is nothing better than retreating to your own private space to relax and restore your energy.

FELTED BOLSTER

An easy and fun felting project.

YARN Ella Rae CLASSIC 100g/3.5oz 200m/219yds		
Col.	No.	Quantity x 100g balls
col A	14	1
col B	05	1
col C	06	1
col D	17	1
col E	12	1

MEASUREMENTS
Before felting:
Length 62cm (24½in)
Width 62cm (24½in)
After felting:
Length 45cm (17¾in)
Width 48cm (19in)

NEEDLES
1 pair 4.50mm (US 7) needles.
TENSION/GAUGE
20 sts and 24 rows measured over 10cm (4in) of St st using 4.50mm (US 7) needles.
ADDITIONAL REQUIREMENTS
Bolster insert: 45cm (17¾in) in length x 48cm (19in) circumference.
2 Tassels

BOLSTER

Using 4.50mm (US 7) needles and col A, cast on 98 sts.
Work in St st as foll:
Col A work 3 cm.
Col B work 6 cm.
Col C work 2 cm.
Col D work 2 cm.
Col B work 6 cm.
Col C work 2 cm.
Col E work 10 cm.
Col C work 2 cm.
Col B work 6 cm.
Col D work 2 cm.
Col C work 2 cm.
Col B work 6 cm.
Col A work 3 cm, ending on a WS row.
Cast off.

ENDS (make 2)

Using 4.50mm (US 7) needles and col A, cast on 90 sts.
St st 4 rows.
Row 5 * K2tog, k1; rep from * to end. (60 sts)
St st 3 rows.
Row 9 * K2tog, k1; rep from * to end. (40 sts)
P 1 row.
Row 11 * K2tog, k1; rep from * to last st, k1. (27 sts)
P 1 row.
Row 13 * K2tog, k1; rep from * to end. (18 sts)
P 1 row.
Row 15 * K2tog; rep from * to end. (9 sts)
Break off yarn, leaving enough length to sew seam.
Thread yarn through rem sts and pull through to secure.
Sew seam using edge to edge st (see method on page 151).

MAKING UP

Felt all pieces separately (see method on page 152).
Fold piece in half width-wise and sew seam to form a tube.
Sew one end into place, then place bolster insert and sew other end into place. Sew a tassel to each end.

Felting is fun and easy~ experiment with colors to complement your own color scheme.

TEXTURED CUSHION

This simple pattern is worked with three colors and a pretty textured stitch.

YARN Ella Rae CLASSIC 100g/3.5oz 200m/219yds			NEEDLES 1 pair 4.50mm (US 7) needles.
Col.	No.	Quantity x 100g balls	
col A	12	1	TENSION/GAUGE
col B	24	1	16 sts and 22 rows measured over 10cm (4in)
col C	19	1	of pattern using 4.50mm (US 7) needles.

MEASUREMENTS
45cm x 45cm (17¾in x 17¾in)

ADDITIONAL REQUIREMENTS
Cushion insert:
45cm x 45cm (17¾in x 17¾in)

Pattern Repeat

Row 1 (RS) Col A, K1, * p1, K1B; rep from * to last st, k1.

Row 2 Col A Knit.

Row 3 Col B, K1 * K1B, p1; rep from * to last st, k1.

Row 4 Col B Knit.

Rows 5+6 Col C, rep rows 1+2.

Rows 7+8 Col A, rep rows 3+4.

Rows 9+10 Col B, rep rows 1+2.

Rows 11+12 Col C, rep rows 3+4.

Repeat these 12 rows.

CUSHION (Make 2)

Using 4.50mm (US 7) needles and col A, cast on 72 sts.

Knit 1 row.

Cont working in pattern repeat until piece measures 45cm (17¾in), ending on either row 2 or row 8.

Cast off.

MAKING UP

Using edge to edge st (see method **on page 151**), sew along three sides. Cushion insert and sew rem seam.

Handy Tip

Try a combination of soft grays or brights to add a special touch to a room.

Trellis Stitch Pillow

Textured Cushion

Felted Bolter

Set the mood for relaxation with an abundance of pillows in calming tones and textures.

Textured Cushion and Trellis Stitch Pillow

TRELLIS STITCH PILLOW

Inspired by Indian mirror work, this pretty pillow will add something special to any room.

YARN Ella Rae CLASSIC			MEASUREMENTS	ADDITIONAL REQUIREMENTS
100g/3.5oz	200m/219yds		Width 25cm (9¾in)	4 beads.
Col.	No.	Quantity x 100g balls	Length 40cm (15¾in)	Cushion/pillow insert:
col A	14	1	NEEDLES	25cm x 40cm (9¾in x 15¾in)
col B	05	1	1 pair 4.50mm (US 7) needles.	SPECIAL ABBREVIATIONS
col C	24	1	TENSION/GAUGE	mb (make bobble) [K1,p1,k1,p1] all into next
col D	26	1	20 sts and 24 rows measured	st, turn, pass 2nd, 3rd and 4th sts over
col E	35	1	over 10cm (4in) of St st using	1st st on left-hand needle (bobble complete).
			4.50mm (US 7) needles.	Using col B knit this st.

Pull up loop

Insert point of right-hand needle upward under the 2 strands in front of the sl sts and knit the next st, then lift the 2 strands off over the point of the right-hand needle.

Trellis Stitch

Row 1 (WS) Using col B K1, p3, * keeping yarn at front of work sl 3 purlwise, p3; rep from * to last st, k1.
Row 2 Using col B P1, k3, * keeping yarn at back of work sl 3 purlwise, k3; rep from * to last st, p1.
Row 3 Using col A K1, p3, * k3, p3; rep from * to last st, k1.
Row 4 Using col A P1, k3, * p3, k3; rep from * to last st, p1.
Row 5 Using col A K5, * pull up loop, k5; rep from * to end.
Row 6 As row 3.
Row 7 Using col B P1, * keeping yarn at front sl 3 purlwise, p3; rep from * to last 4 sts, sl 3 purlwise, p1.
Row 8 Using col B K1, * keeping yarn at back sl 3 purlwise, k3; rep from * to last 4 sts, sl 3 purlwise, k1.
Row 9 As row 4.
Row 10 As row 3.
Row 11 Using col A K2, * pull up loop, k5; rep from * to last 3 sts, pull up loop, k2.
Row 12 As row 4.
Rep these 12 rows.

Moss Stitch

Row 1 K1 * p1, k1; rep from * to end.
Repeat this row.

FRONT

Using 4.50mm (US 7) needles and col A, cast on 51 sts.
Work 4cm (1½in) in Moss st, ending on a RS row.
Using col B, work 3 rows St st beg with a k row.
Next row (RS) * Col B k4, col C mb; rep from * to last 5 sts, using col B k5.

Work in color sequence as foll:
col B, purl 1 row.
col A, knit 1 row.
col D, purl 1 row.
col D, knit 1 row.
col C, purl 1 row.
* col C k1, col B k1; rep from * to end.
col C, purl 1 row.
col A, knit 1 row.
col A, purl 1 row.
col E, knit 1 row.
col C, purl 1 row.
col C, knit 1 row.
col C, purl 1 row.
* col E k1, col C k1; rep,from * to end.
* col E p1, col C p1; rep from * to end.
col C, St st 4 rows, dec 1 st on last row worked. (50 sts)

Picot Stripe

Row 1 (RS) Using col D, k4 * (k1, yf, k1, yf, k1, yf, k1) all into next st, k9; rep from * to last 5 sts, k5.
Row 2 Using col D, knit.
Row 3 Using col C, k3, * k2tog, k5, sl1, k 1, psso, k7; rep from * to last 4 sts, k4.
Row 4 Using col C, p4, * p2togtbl, p1, sl1 wyif, p1, p2tog, p7; rep from * to last 3 sts, p3.
Row 5 Using col C, k3, * k2tog, sl1 wyib, sl1, k1, psso, k7; rep from * to last 4 sts, k4.
Row 6 Using col C, purl 8.
Using col A, work 9 rows in St st, increasing 2 sts on last row worked. (53 sts)
Cont working in Trellis stitch until length measures 40cm (15¾in) from beg, ending on either a row 6 or row 12 of pattern repeat. Cast off.

BACK
Using 4.50mm (US 7) needles and col A, cast on 51 sts.
Work in St st until length measures same as front.
Cast off.

MAKING UP
Embroider circles of Satin st in col D (large circle) and col E (small circle). Sew beads into center of large circles.
Using edge to edge st (see method on page 151), sew along three sides.
Insert pillow and sew rem seam.

FELTED PERSIAN SLIPPERS

These slippers are fun and quick to make. Try sewing some jewel-like beads as an alternative to embroidery.

YARN Ella Rae CLASSIC
100g/3.5oz   200m/219yds

Col. No.	Quantity x 100g balls
25	1

Approx 100cm (39½in) lengths of the foll col's 18, 27 and 30 or alternatively use embroidery thread.

MEASUREMENTS
One size, to fit average adult.

NEEDLES
1 pair 4.50mm (US 7) needles.

TENSION/GAUGE
20 sts and 24 rows measured over 10cm (4in) of St st using 4.50mm (US 7) needles.

SLIPPERS

SIDES (make 2)
Using 4.50mm (US 7) needles, cast on 16 sts.
Work 16cm (6¼in) st st, ending on a WS row. Leave sts on end of needle, break yarn. Make second side the same.

TOP
With RS facing, knit across top of both side pieces. (32 sts)
Purl 1 row.
(RS) (inc) K1, m1, k to last st, m1, k1. (34 sts)
Purl 1 row.
Rep last 2 rows, twice more. (38 sts)
Cont working straight until length measures 23cm (9in), ending on a WS row. (Adjust length here to make size smaller or larger)
Next row (RS) (dec) Dec 1 st each end next row, then 1 st each end every foll alt row, 6 times more. (24 sts)
Dec 1 st each end next 2 rows. (20 sts)
(WS) P2tog across row. (10 sts)
(RS) K2tog across row. (5 sts)
Break yarn and thread through sts to secure.

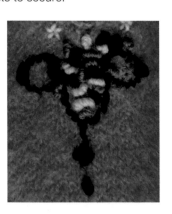

SOLE
Using 4.50mm (US 7) needles, cast on 18 sts.
Knit 1 row.
Purl 1 row.
Next row (RS) (inc) K1, m1, k to last st, m1, k1.
Purl 1 row.
Rep last 2 rows, twice more. (24 sts)
Cont working straight until length measures 8cm (3¼in), ending on a WS row.
Next row (RS) (dec) Dec 1 st each end next row, then 1 st each end foll 4th row, once. (20 sts)
Cont working straight until length measures 13cm (5in), ending on a WS row. (Adjust length here to make size smaller or larger)
Next row (RS) (inc) K1, m1, k to last st, m1, k1.
Purl 1 row.
Rep last 2 rows, twice more. (26 sts)
Cont working straight until length measures 20cm (8in), ending on a WS row.
Next row (RS) (dec) Dec 1 st each end next row, then 1 st each end foll alt rows, 6 times more. (12 sts)
Dec 1 st each end foll 3 rows. (6 sts)
Cast off.
Repeat for second slipper.

MAKING UP
Felt all pieces separately (see method **on page** 152).
Sew back seam of sides tog.
With RS facing, sew soles to top.
Using the photograph as a guide, embroider onto top, using French knots and simple embroidery stitches.

BASKET WEAVE THROW

This complicated looking throw couldn't be simpler to knit. Worked in knit and purl only, it has a stunning effect.

YARN Ella Rae CLASSIC HEATHERS
100g/3.5oz 200m/219yds

Col. No.	Quantity x 100g balls
122	10

MEASUREMENTS
Width approx 115cm (45¼in)
Length approx 130cm (51¼in)

NEEDLES
1 pair 4.50mm (US 7) needles.
TENSION/GAUGE
20 sts and 24 rows measured over 10cm (4in) of St st using 4.50mm (US 7) needles.

NOTE
Circular needle is used to hold the large number of sts. Throw is worked in rows, not rounds.

THROW

Using 4.50mm (US 7) circular needles, cast on 300 sts.
Work 12 rows in Garter St (knit all rows).

Pattern Repeat

Row 1 (RS) K10 sts, * k20, [k2,p2] 5 times; rep from * 6 times, k10.
Row 2 K10, * [k2,p2] 5 times, p20; rep from * 6 times, k10.
Row 3 As row 1.
Row 4 As row 2.
Row 5 K10, * p20, [k2,p2] 5 times; rep from * 6 times, k10.
Row 6 K10, * [k2,p2] 5 times, k20; rep from * 6 times, k10.
Row 7 As row 5.
Row 8 As row 6.
Repeat last 8 rows twice more.
Row 25 K10, * [k2,p2] 5 times, k20; rep from * 6 times, k10.
Row 26 K10, * p20, [k2,p2] 5 times; rep from * 6 times, k10.
Row 27 As row 25.
Row 28 As row 26.
Row 29 K10, * [k2,p2] 5 times, p20; rep from * 6 times, k10.
Row 30 K10, * k20, [k2,p2] 5 times; rep from * 6 times, k10.
Row 31 As row 29.
Row 32 As row 30.
Repeat last 8 rows twice more.

These 48 rows set pattern.
Cont working in pattern as set until length measures approx 126cm (49½in) (ending on either row 24 or 48 of pattern repeat). Work 12 rows in Garter st. Cast off.

Handy Tip

When working on large projects, it is often easier to work with circular needles that have enough length to hold the number of stitches than to try to crowd all the stitches onto straight needles, which make it tight and uncomfortable to knit.

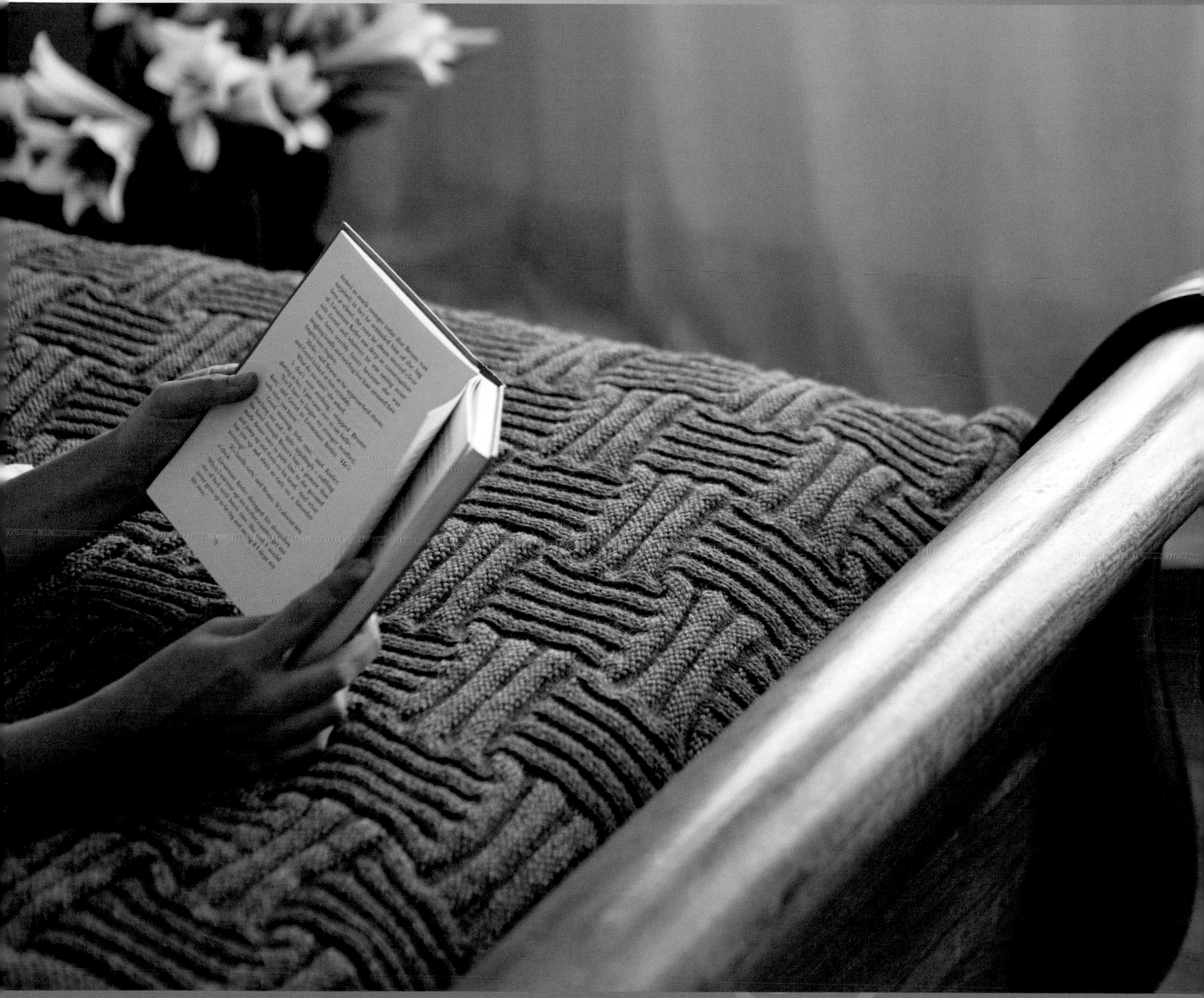

CABLE HOT-WATER-BOTTLE COVER

This simple cover is suitable for a beginner knitter.

YARN Ella Rae CLASSIC
100g/3.5oz 200m/219yds

Col. No.	Quantity x 100g balls
59	1

MEASUREMENTS
Width 20cm (8in)
Height 30cm (11¾in)

NEEDLES
1 pair 4.50mm (US 7) needles.

TENSION/GAUGE
20 sts and 24 rows measured over 10cm (4in) of St st using 4.50mm (US 7) needles.

SPECIAL ABBREVIATIONS
C4F or C4B (Cable 4 Front or Cable 4 Back) slip next 2 sts onto cable needle and hold at front (or back) of work, knit next 2 sts from left-hand needle, then knit sts from cable needle.

FRONT AND BACK

Using 4.50mm (US 7) needles, cast on 47 sts.

Establishment rows

Row 1 (RS) P3, [k8,p3] 4 times.

Row 2 Inc 1 st, k2, [p8,k3] 3 times, p8, k2, inc 1 st. [49 sts]

Row 3 Inc 1 st, p3, [C4F,C4B,p3] 3 times, C4F, C4B, p3, inc 1 st. [51 sts]

Row 4 Inc 1 st, k4, [p8,k3] 3 times, p8, k4, inc 1 st. [53 sts]

Row 5 Inc 1 st, p5, [k8,p3] 3 times, k8, p5, inc 1 st. [55 sts]

** Row 6 K7, [p8,k3] 3 times, p8, k7.

Row 7 P7, [C4F,C4B,p3] 3 times, C4F,C4B, p7.

Row 8 K7, [p8,k3] 3 times, p8, k7.

Row 9 P7, [k8,p3] 3 times, k8, p7. ***

Cont working from ** to *** in repeat until length measures 18cm (7in), ending on a WS row, dec 1 st on last row worked. [54 sts]

Row 1 (RS) Purl.

Row 2 K1, * [k1,p1,k1] into next st, p3tog; rep from * to last st, k1.

Row 3 Purl.

Row 4 K1, *p3tog, [k1,p1,k1] into next st; rep from * to last st, k1.

These 4 rows form patt repeat.

Cont working in patt rep until length measures 22cm (8¾in), ending on a WS row.

(RS)(eyelet row) P3, [yfrn,p2tog,p4] 8 times, p3.

(WS) Knit.

(RS) K2, * p2, k2; rep from * to end.

(WS) P2, * k2, p2; rep from * to end.

These 2 rows form rib.

Cont working in rib, until length measures 32cm (12½in) from beg, ending on a WS row. Cast off in rib.

MAKING UP

Sew front and back pieces tog using edge to edge st (or method preferred).

Using 6 strands of yarn, braid a length of cord and thread through eyelets.

Handy Tip

Never join in a new yarn in the center of a row unless working a picture knit. Join a new yarn at the beginning of a row, leaving a tail to be darned in later. If you must join a new yarn in the middle of a row, leave enough of a tail from the old yarn and the same length from the new yarn at the back of the work and darn them in later. Never knot the ends together.

Snuggle up on a cold night with these stylish hot-water bottle covers

FELTED POUCH

This sweet little pouch is felted then decorated with beads and embroidery.

YARN Ella Rae CLASSIC
100g/3.5oz 200m/219yds

Col. No.	Quantity x 100g balls
06	1

MEASUREMENTS
Finished 10cm x 15cm (4in x 6in)
NEEDLES
1 pair 4.50mm (US 7) needles.

TENSION/GAUGE
20 sts and 24 rows measured over 10cm (4in) of St st using 4.50mm (US 7) needles.
ADDITIONAL REQUIREMENTS
Glass beads
Embroidery thread
Cord

FRONT and BACK (Make 2)

Using 4.50mm (US 7) needles, cast on 28 sts.
Work 16cm (6¼in) in St st, beg with a RS row and ending on a WS row.

MAKING UP

Felt pieces separately (see method **on page** 152).
Sew sides and bottom edges tog.

Cut small slits in fabric approx 1cm (½in) below cast off edge and approx 1.5cm (¾in) apart.
Thread cord through slits.
Sew a double row of glass beads around top edge of pouch. See page 147 for embroidery design and stitch guide.

BLACKBERRY STITCH HOT-WATER-BOTTLE COVER

YARN Ella Rae CLASSIC
100g/3.5oz 200m/219yds

Col. No.	Quantity x 100g balls
99	1

MEASUREMENTS
Width 20cm (8in)
Height 30cm (11¾in)

NEEDLES
1 pair 4.50mm (US 7) needles.
TENSION/GAUGE
20 sts and 24 rows measured over 10cm (4in) of St st using 4.50mm (US 7) needles.

FRONT

Using 4.50mm (US 7) needles, cast on 36 sts.
Working in St st, beg with a knit row, inc 1 st each end next row, then 1 st each end every foll row 3 times more. [44 sts] **
Cont working straight until length measures 4cm (1½in), ending on a WS row.
Row 1 (RS) K11, p22, k11.
Row 2 P11, k1, * [k1,p1,k1] into next st, p3tog; rep from * 5 times, k1, p11.
Row 3 As row 1.
Row 4 P11, k1, * p3tog, [k1,p1,k1] into next st; rep from * 5 times, k1, p11.
Rep these 4 rows until length measures 26cm (10¼in) from beg, ending on a WS row.
Cont working in St st, beg with a k row, until length measures 27cm (10½in), ending on a WS row. *** Next row (RS) Dec 1 st each end next row, then each end foll alt rows 3 times more.
(36 sts)

Next row (WS) K2, * yf, k2tog; rep from * to end.
Change to 4.00mm needles.
(RS) * K2, p2; rep from * to end.
(WS) * K2, p2; rep from * to end.
These 2 rows form rib.
Cont working in rib until length measures 16cm (6¼in), ending on a WS row. Cast off in rib.

BACK

Work as for front to **.
Cont working in St st until length measures 27cm (10½in), ending on a WS row.
Cont working as for front from *** to end.

MAKING UP

Sew front and back pieces tog using edge to edge st (or method preferred).
Using 6 strands of yarn, braid a length of cord and thread through eyelets.

This felted pouch would make a lovely gift for a special friend.

106

103

112

114

116

108

100

113

120

118

102

122

94

A Room for Little Ones

A special place where children retreat to play and feel free to be themselves, a place for doll parties with friends, dress-ups, and games to play ~ this room will hold sweet memories.

Create precious things for the
little ones we love ~ they will be
treasured forever.

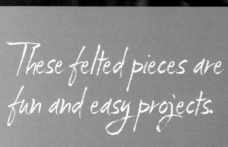

These felted pieces are fun and easy projects.

FELTED BOOTS

These funky little boots are great for slipping on in the morning when the weather turns cool.

YARN Ella Rae CLASSIC
100g/3.5oz 200m/219yds

Col. No.   Quantity x 100g balls
93   2

MEASUREMENTS

Length approx 20cm (8in)

Height approx 15cm (6in)

Length can be altered to make a smaller or bigger size boot.

NEEDLES

1 pair 6.50mm (US 10½) needles.

TENSION/GAUGE

20 sts and 24 rows measured over 10cm (4in) of St st using 4.50mm (US 7) needles.

SPECIAL ABBREVIATIONS

m1 (make 1) pick up the st lying between the st just worked and the next st and knit it.

BASE

Using 6.50mm (US 10½) needles and 2 strands of yarn, cast on 10 sts.

Knit 1 row.

Purl 1 row.

Next row (RS) (inc) K1, m1, k to last st, m1, k1.

Purl 1 row.

Rep last 2 rows twice more. (16 sts)

Cont working straight until length measures 6cm (2½in), ending on a WS row.

Next row (RS) (dec) Dec 1 st each end next row, then 1 st each end foll 4th row once. (12 sts)

Cont working straight until length measures 12cm (4¾in) (or length desired), ending on a WS row.

(RS) (inc) K1, m1, k to last st, m1, k1.

Purl 1 row.

Rep last 2 rows twice more. (18 sts)

Cont working straight until length measures 18cm (7in) (or length desired), ending on a WS row.

Next row (RS) (dec) Dec 1 st each end next row, then 1 st each end foll alt rows 5 times, then 1 st each end every foll row twice. (4 sts) Cast off.

Place a marker at center of the heel.

SIDES

Using 6.50mm (US 10½) needles and 2 strands of yarn, cast on 6 sts.

Cont working in St st until length measures same as the base, measured from the marker at the heel, around the outside of the base and finishing at the marker.

Sew side piece to base, beg and ending at the marker at center of heel. Sew seam.

TOP FRONT PIECE

Toe

Using 6.50mm (US 10½) needles and 2 strands of yarn, cast on 4 sts.

Knit 1 row.

Purl 1 row.

Next row (RS) (inc) Inc 1 st each end next row, then 1 st each end foll alt rows 6 times more. (18 sts)

Cont working straight until length measures 14cm (5½in) (or length desired), ending on a WS row.

Place a marker each end last row worked.

Cont working straight for a further 12cm (4¾in), ending on a WS row.

Next row (RS) * K2, yf, k2tog; rep from * to last 2 sts, k2.

Purl 1 row.

Knit 1 row.

Purl 1 row.

Cast off.

Sew top of boot to base and sides, beg at toe and ending at marker either side.

Side Gusset (make 2)

With WS facing, using 6.50mm (US 10½) needles and 2 strands of yarn, pickup and knit 4 sts along side edge from marker on the top front piece towards back of boot.

Work in St st until length measures 12cm (4¾n), ending on a WS row.

Next row (RS) K1, yf, k2tog, k1.

Purl 1 row.

Knit 1 row.

Purl 1 row.

Cast off.

Sew one edge of gusset to front piece.

Heel and Back Piece

With WS facing, using 6.50mm (US 10½) needles and
2 strands of yarn, pickup and knit 30 sts beg side gusset,
along edge to side gusset on other side of boot.
Cont working in St st until length measures 12cm (4¾in),
ending on a WS row.
Next row (RS) * K2, yf, k2tog; rep from * to last 2 sts, k2.
Purl 1 row.
Knit 1 row.
Purl 1 row.
Cast off.

Sew back piece and gusset seam.

MAKING UP

Felt the boots using method on page 152.
Cord Make 2 lengths of braided cord approx 30cm (11¾in)
long (or length desired). Thread the cord through the eyelets
along top of boot, beginning and ending at center front.
Make 4 small pompoms, attach a pompom to each
end of cord. ❏

BABY SLIPPERS

These felted slippers are quick and easy, and they make a great gift.

YARN Ella Rae CLASSIC
100g/3.5oz   200m/219yds

Col.	No.	Quantity x 100g balls
col A	59	1
col B	54	1

MEASUREMENTS
12–18 months.
Length approx 12cm (4¾in)
Width approx 7cm (2¾in)

NEEDLES
1 pair 8.00mm (US 11) needles.

TENSION/GAUGE
12 sts and 16 rows measured over 10cm (4in) of St st using 8.00mm (US 11) needles, using 2 strands of yarn.

SLIPPERS

Base Using 8.00mm (US 11) needles and 2 strands of col A, cast on 9 sts.
Knit 1 row.
Next row (inc) Inc 1 st each end next row, then every foll rows, twice. (15 sts)
St st 14 rows.
Next row (RS) (dec) Dec 1 st each end next row, then 1 st each end foll 4th row. (11 sts)
St st 7 rows.
Cast off 2 sts at beg next 2 rows.
Cast off rem sts.

Top Using 8.00mm (US 11) needles and 2 strands of col A, cast on 9 sts.
Knit 1 row.
Inc 1 st each end next row, then 1 st each end foll rows, twice. (15 sts)
Next row (RS) K4 sts, refer to graph on page 147, k4 sts. Work 1 row of graph.
Cont to work next 6 graph rows as set, working St st on either side.
St st 2 rows.
Sides (WS) P5 sts, cast off 5 sts, p to end.
(RS) K5 sts, leave rem 5 sts unworked.
St st 18 rows. Cast off.
With RS facing, rejoin yarn to rem sts.
Work second side to match for side.

MAKING UP

Sew seam at back. Sew top of slipper to base, using edge to edge st.
Felt using instructions on page 152. ❏

FELTED BAG

This simple bag is easy to knit and felt. Embellish with felted wcrochet flowers.

YARN Ella Rae CLASSIC			NEEDLES
100g/3.5oz 200m/219yds			1 pair 4.50mm (US 7) needles.
Col.	**No.**	**Quantity x 100g balls**	1 4.50mm (US G) crochet hook.
col A	34	1	**TENSION/GAUGE**
col B	93	1	20 sts and 24 rows measured over 10cm (4in)

MEASUREMENTS
of St st using 4.50mm (US 7) needles.
Width approx 19cm (7½in)
Height approx 15cm (6in)
Depth approx 4cm (1½in)

FRONT and BACK (make 2)
Using 4.50mm (US 7) needles, cast on 48 sts.
Work in St st for 25cm (10in), ending on a purl row. Cast off.

GUSSET (make 2)
Using 4.50mm (US 7) needles, cast on 14 sts.
Work in St st for 25cm (10in), ending on a purl row. Cast off.

BASE (make 1)
Using 4.50mm (US 7) needles, cast on 14 sts.
Work in St st for 24cm (9½in), ending on a purl row. Cast off.

HANDLE (make 1)
Using 4.50mm (US 7) needles, cast on 14 sts.
Work in St st for 40cm (15¾in), ending on a purl row. Cast off.

FLOWERS (make 3)
Using 4.50mm (US G) crochet hook, col B and 2 strands of yarn tog, make 28 ch, turn, * [dc into first ch, 1ch, yon, 1 tr, 1 ch, 1 tr, 1ch, 1tr, 1 ch, 1 dc] all into first ch, miss 2 ch **; rep from * to ** 8 times more.

The flower will naturally curl. Arrange into flower shape and sew to secure.

MAKING UP
Fold handle in half to form a hollow tube.
Sew seam.
Lay front and back pieces one on top of the other so that WS are tog. Sew a gusset piece to either side of front and back pieces, with RS facing leaving raw edges on the outside of work.
Sew base the same way to front and back, the sew either end to gusset at side.
Sew handle to top edge of gusset pieces on both sides.

Felt the bag and flowers separately using method on page 152.
Sew flowers onto front of bag. ❏

When I was about ten I loved to knit clothes for my dolls. This was the start of my passion for knitting. My daughter now has this precious collection.

105

JACQUELINE AND MADELEINE DOLLS

These beautiful dolls will be treasured forever.

YARN Ella Rae CLASSIC		
100g/3.5oz 200m/219yds		
Col. No.	Quantity x 100g balls	
Jacqueline		
col A 06	1	
col B 59	1	
Madeleine		
col A 06	1	
col B 97	1	
col C 59	1	

MEASUREMENTS
Height approx 38cm (15in)
NEEDLES
1 pair 4.50mm (US 7) needles.
Madeleine
1 pair 4.00mm (US 6) needles.
1 cable needle
TENSION/GAUGE
20 sts and 24 rows measured over 10cm (4in) of St st using 4.50mm (US 7) needles.

ADDITIONAL REQUIREMENTS
Polyester Fiberfill
Jacqueline
3 small buttons
Fabric dress
SPECIAL ABBREVIATIONS
C4F (Cable 4 Front) Slip next 2 sts onto cable needle, leave at front of work, k next 2 sts from left-hand needle then k 2 sts from cable needle.

BODY

Legs (make 2)

Using 4.50mm (US 7) needles and col A, cast on 10 sts.
Row 1 Knit.
Row 2 Purl.
Row 3 K1, m1 (pickup st lying between sts and knit into it), knit to last 2 sts, m1, k2. (12 sts)
Row 4 Purl.
Row 5 As row 3. (14 sts)
Row 6 Purl.
Row 7 As row 3. (16 sts)
Row 8 Purl.
Row 9 As row 3. (18 sts)
Row 10 Purl.
Cont working in St st until length measures 20cm (8in), ending on a WS row. Break off yarn and hold at end of needle. Make other leg the same.

Bodice

Knit across top of both legs. (36 sts)
Cont in St st until bodice length measures 18cm (7in), ending on a WS row. Cast off.

Head (make 2)

Using 4.50mm (US 7) needles and col A, cast on 12 sts.
Knit 1 row.
Purl 1 row.
Dec 1 st each end foll 2 rows. (8 sts)
Knit 1 row.
Inc 1 st each end next 2 rows. (12 sts)
Purl 1 row.
Inc 1 st each end next row, then on foll alt row, once. (16 sts)
St st 7 rows.
Dec 1 st each end next row, then on foll alt row, once. (12 sts)
Purl 1 row.
Dec 1 st each end next 3 rows. (6 sts)
P2tog, 3 times. (3 sts) Cast off.

Hands and Arms (make 2)

Using 4.50mm (US 7) needles and col A, cast on 8 sts.
Knit 1 row.
Purl 1 row.
Inc 1 st each end next row, then on foll alt row, once. (12 sts)
Cont in St st until length measures 20cm (8in). Cast off.

Fold legs and bodice in half and sew tog using edge to edge st (or method preferred).
Fold arms in half and sew. Sew head pieces tog.
Stuff all pieces sufficiently with polyester fiberfill and sew head and arms on to bodice.

Felt body using instructions on page 152. ❏

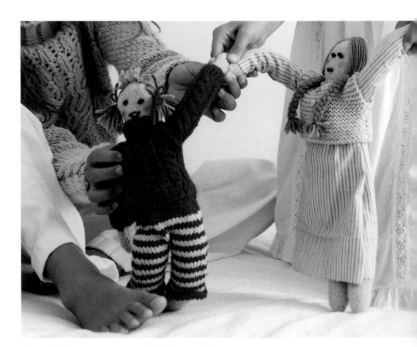

Madeleine (LEFT) *& Jacqueline* (RIGHT)

CLOTHES

Jaqueline

TOP

Back

Using 4.50mm (US 7) needles, cast on 30 sts.
Cont working in Garter st (knit all rows) until length measures 10cm (4in), ending on a WS row.
Cast off.

Front

Work as for back.

MAKING UP

With RS tog, sew back and front tog leaving an opening of approx 8cm (3¼in) for the neck and approx 6cm (2½in) along the side seams for the arms.

Sew 3 buttons down the center front at regular intervals. ❏

Madeleine

PANTS (make 2)

Using 4.50mm (US 7) needles and col B, cast on 24 sts.
(RS) * K2, pass 2nd st over 1st st; rep from * to end.
Purl 1 row.
Change to col C, k 1 row, p 1 row.
Change to col B, k1 row, p 1 row.
Repeat last 4 rows, 4 times, then work 2 more rows in col B.
Break off yarn and hold at end of needle.
Make other leg the same.
Using col C, k across sts of both legs. (24 sts)
P 1 row.
Change to col B, k 1 row, p 1 row.
Change to col C, k 1 row, p 1 row.
Repeat last 4 rows, once more, then work 8 rows in col B.
Cast off. ❏

SWEATER

Front

Using 4.00mm (US 6) needles and col B, cast on 25 sts.
(RS) K1 * p1, k1; rep from * to end.
(WS) P1 * k1, p1; rep from * to end.
These 2 rows form rib.
Cont working in rib until length measures 2cm (¾in), ending on a WS row, inc 1 st on last row worked. (26 sts)
Change to 4.50mm (US 7) needles.
Row 1 (RS) K2, p1, k4, p1, k2, p1, k4, p1, k2, p1, k4, p1, k2.
Row 2 P2, k1, p4, k1, p2, k1, p4, k1, p2, k1, p4, k1, p2.

Row 3 K2, p1, C4F, p1, k2, p1, C4F, p1, k2, p1, C4F, p1, k2.
Row 4 As row 2.
These 4 rows form pattern repeat.
Cont working in patt until length measures 12cm (4¾in), ending on a WS row.
(RS) Cast off 7 sts at beg next 2 rows. (13 sts)
Cont working in k1, p1 rib on these 13 center sts for 3cm (11¼in), ending on a WS row.
Cast off in rib.

Back

Work as for front.

Sleeves

Using 4.00mm (US 6) needles and col B, cast on 17 sts.
(RS) K1 * p1, k1; rep from * to end.
(WS) P1 * k1, p1; rep from * to end.
These 2 rows form rib.
Cont working in rib until length measures 2cm (¾in), ending on a WS row, inc 1 st on last row worked. (18 sts)
Change to 4.50mm (US 7) needles.
Row 1 (RS) K2, p1, k4, p1, k2, p1, k4, p1, k2.
Row 2 P2, k1, p4, k1, p2, k1, p4, k1, p2.
Row 3 K2, p1, C4F, p1, k2, p1, C4F, p1, k2.
Row 4 P2, k1, p4, k1, p2, k1, p4, k1, p2.
These 4 rows form pattern repeat.
Cont working in patt until length measures 12cm (4¾in), ending on a WS row.
Cast off. ❏

MAKING UP

Pants Sew inside seams and side seams.
Sweater Sew front and back shoulder seams.
Center sleeves and sew into place.
Sew sleeve and side seams.
Hair Using extra scraps of yarn, cut required lengths and thread through top of head along the seam line. Stitch into place to secure at intervals.

Paint or sew the face on using scraps of yarn. ❏

CABLE & DOUBLE MOSS STITCH SWEATER

A pretty combination of cables, lace and texture.

YARN	Ella Rae AMITY			
100g/3.5oz	182m/200yds			
	A	B	C	D
	3-4	5-6	7-8	9-10 yrs
Chest	61	66	71	76 cm
Col. No.	Quantity x 100g balls			
2	3	4	5	6

NEEDLES
1 pair 4.50mm (US 7) needles.
1 pair 5.00mm (US 8) needles.
1 cable needle.

TENSION/GAUGE
20 sts and 25 rows measured over 10cm (4in) of Double Moss st using 5.00mm (US 9) needles.
23 sts and 25 rows measured over 10cm (4in) of Lace pattern using 5.00mm (US 9) needles.
Cable panel measures approx 5cm (2in).

SPECIAL ABBREVIATION
C2B or C2F (cross 2 back or front) knit into back (or front) of 2nd st on needle, then knit first st, slipping both sts off needle at the same time.
MEASUREMENTS Refer to diagram on page 148.

Chalice Cable

Row 1 (RS) K1, [p2, k2] 3 times, p2, k1.
Row 2 P1, k2, [p2, k2] 3 times, p1.
Rep last 2 rows twice more.
Row 7 * Slip next 4 sts onto cn and hold at back of work, k1, p2, k1 from left-hand needle, then k1, p2, k1 from cn, slip next 4 sts onto cable needle and hold at front of work, k1, p2, k1 from left-hand needle, then k1, p2, k1 from cn.
Row 8 As row 2.
Row 9 As row 1.
Row 10 As row 2.
Repeat these 10 rows.

Double Moss St

Row 1 K1, * p1, k1; rep from * to end.
Row 2 P1, * k1, p1; rep from * to end.
Row 3 As row 2.
Row 4 As row 1.
Repeat these 4 rows.

Bell Lace

Row 1 (RS) K1, p1, k1, * p1, yon, sl 1, k2tog, psso, yfrn, [p1, k1] twice; rep from * to end.
Row 2 P1, k1, p1, * k1, p3, [k1, p1] twice; rep from * to end.
Repeat last 2 rows twice more.
Row 7 K1, k2tog, * yfrn, [p1, k1] twice, p1, yon, sl 1, k2tog, psso; rep from * to last 8 sts, yfrn, [p1, k1] twice, p1, yon, sl 1, k1, psso, k1.
Row 8 P3, * [k1, p1] twice, k1, p3; rep from * to end.
Repeat last 2 rows twice more.
Repeat these 12 rows.

FRONT

Using 5.00mm (US 8) needles cast on 86(90,94,98) sts.

Establishment rows

Row 1 (RS) Work 27(29,31,33) sts in Double Moss st, work row 1 of Chalice Cable panel twice, work 27(29,31,33) sts in Double Moss St.
Row 2 (WS) Work 27(29,31,33) sts in Double Moss st, work row 2 of Chalice Cable panel twice, work 27(29,31,33) sts in Double Moss st. These 2 rows set pattern.

Cont working in pattern as set until length measures 20(22,24,26)cm [8(8¾,9½,10¼) in] from beg, ending on a WS row, size A only dec 3 sts on last row worked, sizes B, C and D inc 1(5,9) sts on last row worked. [83(91,99,107) sts]
Work 12 rows in Bell Lace pattern.

Shape armholes (RS) Cast off 3 sts, yon, sl 1, k2tog, psso, yfrn, [p1, k1] twice, * p1, yon, sl 1, k2tog, psso, yfrn, [p1, k1] twice; rep from * to end. [80(88,96,104) sts]
(WS) Cast off 3 sts, p3, [k1, p1] twice, * k1, p3, [k1, p1] twice; rep from * to last 5 sts, k1, p3, k1. [77(85,93,101) sts]
(RS) K2tog, p1, k1, * p1, yon, sl 1, k2tog, psso, yfrn, [p1, k1] twice; rep from * to last 5 sts, p1, k1, p1, k2tog.
(WS) K2tog, p1, * k1, p3, [k1, p1] twice; rep from * to last 4 sts, k1, p1, k2tog.
(RS) K2tog, * p1, yon, sl 1, k2tog, psso, yfrn, [p1, k1] twice; rep from * to last 7 sts, p1, yon, sl 1, k2tog, psso, yfrn, p1, k2tog.
(WS) K2tog, * p3, [k1, p1] twice, k1; rep from * to last 5 sts, p3, k2tog. [69(77,85,93) sts]
(RS) * P1, yon, sl 1, k2tog, psso, yfrn, [p1, k1] twice; rep from * to last 5 sts, p1, yon, sl 1, k2tog, psso, yfrn, p1.
(WS) * K1, p3, [k1, p1] twice; rep from * to last 5 sts, k1, p3, k1.
*** (RS) * [p1, k1] twice, p1, yon, sl 1, k2tog, psso, yfrn; rep from * to last 5 sts, [p1, k1] twice, p1.
(WS) * [k1, p1] twice, k1, p3; rep from * to last 5 sts, [k1, p1] twice, k1.
Rep last 2 rows twice more.
(RS) * P1, yon, sl 1, k2tog, psso, yfrn, [p1, k1] twice; rep from * to last 5 sts, p1, yon, sl 1, k2tog, psso, yfrn, p1.
(WS) * K1, p3, [k1, p1] twice; rep from * to last 5 sts, k1, p3, k1.
Rep last 2 rows twice more.
Cont working from *** to end in repeat until length measures 33(36,39,42)cm, ending on a WS row.
Shape front neck (RS) Patt 28(32,36,40) sts, turn, leave rem sts on a holder.
Work each side of neck separately.
(WS) Cast off 4(4,5,5) sts, patt to end.
Patt 1 row.
(WS) Cast off 3(3,4,5) sts, patt to end.

Patt 1 row.

(WS) Cast off 3(4,3,4) sts, patt to end.

Shape shoulder (RS) Cast off 6(7,8,9) sts at beg next row, then at beg foll alt row once.

Patt 1 row.

Cast off rem 6(7,8,8) sts.

With RS facing, cast off 13 center sts, patt to end.

Patt 1 row.

(RS) Cast off 4(4,5,5) sts, patt to end.

Patt 1 row.

(RS) Cast off 3(3,4,5) sts, patt to end.

Patt 1 row.

(RS) Cast off 3(4,3,4) sts, patt to end.

Shape shoulder (WS) Cast off 6(7,8,9) sts at beg next row, then beg foll alt row once.

Patt 1 row. Cast off rem 6(7,8,8) sts.

BACK

Using 5.00mm (US 8) needles, cast on 75(81,85,89) sts.

Cont working in Double Moss st until length measures 20(22,24,26)cm [8(8¾,9½,10¼) in] from beg, ending on a WS row, inc 8(10,14,18) sts evenly across last row worked. [83(91,99,107) sts]

Work 12 rows in Bell Lace pattern.

Shape armholes (RS) Cast off 3 sts, yon, sl 1, k2tog, psso, yfrn, [p1, k1] twice, * p1, yon, sl 1, k2tog, psso, yfrn, [p1, k1] twice; rep from * to end. [80(88,96,104) sts]

(WS) Cast off 3 sts, p3, [k1, p1] twice, * k1, p3, [k1, p1] twice; rep from * to last 5 sts, k1, p3, k1. [77(85,93,101) sts]

(RS) K2tog, p1, k1, * p1, yon, sl 1, k2tog, psso, yfrn, [p1, k1] twice; rep from * to last 5 sts, p1, k1, p1, k2tog.

(WS) K2tog, p1, * k1, p3, [k1, p1] twice; rep from * to last 4 sts, k1, p1, k2tog.

(RS) K2tog, * p1, yon, sl 1, k2tog, psso, yfrn, [p1, k1] twice; rep from * to last 7 sts, p1, yon, sl 1, k2tog, psso, yfrn, p1, k2tog.

(WS) K2tog, * p3, [k1, p1] twice, k1; rep from * to last 5 sts, p3, k2tog. [69(77,85,93) sts]

(RS) * P1, yon, sl 1, k2tog, psso, yfrn, [p1, k1] twice; rep from * to last 5 sts, p1, yon, sl 1, k2tog, psso, yfrn, p1.

(WS) * K1, p3, [k1, p1] twice; rep from * to last 5 sts, k1, p3, k1.

*** (RS) * [p1, k1] twice, p1, yon, sl 1, k2tog, psso, yfrn; rep from * to last 5 sts, [p1, k1] twice, p1.

(WS) * [k1, p1] twice, k1, p3; rep from * to last 5 sts, [k1, p1] twice, k1.

Rep last 2 rows twice more.

(RS) * P1, yon, sl 1, k2tog, psso, yfrn, [p1, k1] twice; rep from * to last 5 sts, p1, yon, sl 1, k2tog, psso, yfrn, p1.

(WS) * K1, p3, [k1, p1] twice; rep from * to last 5 sts, k1, p3, k1.

Rep last 2 rows twice more.

Cont working from *** to end in repeat until length measures same as front to sh sh, ending on a WS row.

Shape shoulders and back neck (RS) Cast off 6(7,8,9) sts, patt 22(25,28,31) sts, turn, leave rem sts on a holder.

(WS) Cast off 5(5,6,7) sts, patt to end.

(RS) Cast off 6(7,8,9) sts, patt to end.

(WS) Cast off 5(6,6,7) sts, patt to end.

(RS) Cast off rem 6(7,8,8) sts.

With RS facing, cast off 13 center sts, patt to end.

(WS) Cast off 6(7,8,9) sts, patt to end.

(RS) Cast off 5(5,6,7) sts, patt to end.

(WS) Cast off 6(7,8,9) sts, patt to end.

(RS) Cast off 5(6,6,7) sts, patt to end.

(WS) Cast off rem 6(7,8,8) sts.

SLEEVES

Using 5.00mm needles, cast on 42(46,50,54) sts.

Establishment rows

Row 1 (RS) Work 13(15,17,19) sts in Double Moss st, work row 1 of Chalice Cable Panel, work 13(15,17,19) sts in Double Moss st.

Row 2 (WS) Work 13(15,17,19) sts in Double Moss st, work row 2 of Chalice Cable Panel, work 13(15,17,19) sts in Double Moss st.

These 2 rows set patt.

Cont working in patt as set, AT THE SAME TIME **shape sides** as foll: Inc 1 st each end foll 12th(14th,14th,16th) rows, 6(6,4,4) times, then on foll 0(0,16th,18th) rows, 0(0,2,2) times. [54(58,62,66) sts, 72(84,88,100) shaping rows]

Cont working straight until length measures 31(35,39,43)cm [12¼(13¾,15¼,17) in], ending on a WS row.

Shape sleeve top (RS) Cast off 4 sts at beg next 2 rows, then 3 sts at beg next 6 rows. [28(32,36,40) sts]

Dec 1 st each end next 4 rows. [20(24,28,32) sts]

Cast off rem sts.

MAKING UP

Press pieces gently on WS, using a warm iron over a damp cloth. Join right shoulder seam.

Collar With RS facing, using 4.50mm (US 7) needles pickup and knit 16(17,18,19) sts along left side front neck, 14(15,16,17) sts across center front, 16(17,18,19) sts along right side front neck, 13(14,15,16) sts along right side back neck, 14(15,16,17) sts across center back neck and 13(14,15,16) sts along left side back neck. [86(92,98,104) sts]

Double Twisted Rib

Row 1 (WS) K2, * p4, k2; rep from * to end.

Row 2 (RS) P2, * C2B, C2F, p2; rep from * to end.

These 2 rows form pattern repeat.

Cont working in twisted rib patt until length measures 8cm (3¼in), ending on a WS row. Cast off.

Join left shoulder and collar seam.

Join side seams. Join sleeve seams.

Center sleeve into armhole and sew into place. ❑

Cable Cot Blanket

Rosebud Crib Blanket

Cable & Garter Stitch
Cot Blanket

Tweed Stitch Blanket

CABLE COT BLANKET

Pom poms and garter stitch give this classic cable blanket a touch of fun.

YARN Ella Rae CLASSIC SUPERWASH
100g/3.5oz   200m/219yds

Col. No.   Quantity x 100g balls
6   4

MEASUREMENTS
Width approx 65cm (25½in)
Length approx 70cm (27½in)

NEEDLES
1 pair 4.50mm (US 7) needles.
1 cable needle.

TENSION/GAUGE
24 sts and 24 rows measured over 10cm (4in) of Cable patt using 4.50mm (US 7) needles.

SPECIAL ABBREVIATIONS
C4B or C4F (Cable 4 Back or Cable 4 Front) — slip next 2 sts onto a cable needle and hold at back (or front) of work, knit next 2 sts from left-hand needle, then knit sts from cable needle.

BLANKET
Using 4.50mm (US 7) needles, cast on 130 sts.
Row 1 (RS) K4, * p2, k10, p2, k4; rep from * to end.
Row 2 P4, * k2, p10, k2, p4; rep from * to end.
Row 3 K4, * p2, C4B, k2, C4F, p2, k4; rep from * to end.
Row 4 As row 2.
These 4 rows form patt repeat.
Cont working in pattern repeat until length measures 70cm (27½in), ending on a WS row, dec 20 sts evenly across last row worked. (110 sts)
(RS) Cont working in garter st, until length measures 85cm (33½in), ending on a WS row.
Picot Point Cast off
Cast off 2 sts, * slip rem st on right-hand needle onto left-hand needle, cast on 2 sts, cast off 4 sts; rep from * to end. Fasten off rem st.

Fold garter st section over, slip st into place.
Make 7 small pompoms and sew to blanket just above picot edge.
Press pieces using a warm iron over a damp cloth. ❑

Handy Tip

An easy way to make small pom poms is to wrap yarn around two fingers. When sufficient yarn is wrapped, securely tie a piece of yarn between the two fingers and pull tight to gather the lengths together. Slip the yarn off fingers and cut ends. Fluff up to form shape, then trim to size.

CABLE AND GARTER STITCH COT BLANKET

This beautiful baby blanket is a stunning mix of cables and garter stitch with a pretty pointed edging and a picot chain added later.

YARN Ella Rae CLASSIC SUPERWASH
100g/3.5oz 200m/219yds
Col. No.   Quantity x 100g balls
7   5
MEASUREMENTS
Width approx 65cm (25½in)
Length approx 78cm (30¾in)
NEEDLES
1 pair 4.50mm (US 7) needles.
1 cable needle.

TENSION/GAUGE
20 sts and 24 rows measured over 10cm of
St st using 4.50mm (US 7) needles.
SPECIAL ABBREVIATIONS
C6F or C6B (cable 6 front or cable 6 back)
— slip next 3 sts onto cable needle and hold
at front (or back) of work, knit next 3 sts
from left-hand needle, then knit sts from
cable needle.

CABLE PATTERN (9sts)
Row 1 (RS) Knit.
Row 2 (and every WS row) Purl.
Row 3 C6F, k3.
Row 5 Knit.
Row 7 K3, C6B.
Row 8 Purl.
These 8 rows form pattern repeat

BLANKET
Using 4.50mm (US 7) needles, cast on 116 sts.
Establishment rows
(RS) K10, * work row 1 of cable pattern,
k20; rep from * twice more, work row 1
of cable pattern, k10.
(WS) K10, * work row 2 of cable pattern,
k20; rep from * twice more, work row 2
of cable pattern, k10.
These 2 rows set pattern repeat.
Cont working in pattern as set until length
measures 65cm (25½in), ending on a
WS row. Cast off.

*A beautiful baby
blanket that you can
throw in the wash,
time and time again.*

Garter St Point Edging
Cast on 2 sts.
Row 1 K2.
Row 2 Yf (to make a st), k2.
Row 3 Yf, k3.
Row 4 Yf, k4.
Row 5 Yf, k5.
Row 6 Yf, k6.
Row 7 Yf, k7.
Row 8 Yf, k8.
Row 9 Yf, k9.
Row 10 Yf, k10.
Row 11 Yf, k11.
Row 12 Yf, k12.
Break yarn and leave on needle. Repeat
this 9 times more. (10 points made)
With RS facing knit across all 10 points.
(130 sts)
Work 9 rows in garter st. Cast off.
Repeat this 3 times more.
Sew each length to blanket, beg with the 2
sides first, then the top and bottom edges.
Press using a warm iron over a damp cloth.

Picot Point Chain
Cast on 5 sts. * Cast off 4 sts, slip rem st
on right-hand needle, cast on 4 sts; rep
from * until chain is long enough to
fit around edge of point on blanket.
Sew into place. ❏

ROSEBUD CRIB BLANKET

A repeat pattern of little chain stitches forms the diamonds on this beautiful baby blanket.

YARN Ella Rae CLASSIC
100g/3.5oz 200m/219yds

Col. No.	Quantity x 100g balls
9	5

Lengths of pink and red yarn for embroidering rosebuds.
Classic no's 73 and 21 were used.

MEASUREMENTS
Width approx 60cm (23½in)
Length approx 96cm (37¾in)

NEEDLES
1 pair 4.50mm (US 7) needles.
1 embroidery needle.

TENSION/GAUGE
20 sts and 24 rows measured over 10cm (4in) of St st using 4.50mm (US 7) needles.

ADDITIONAL REQUIREMENTS
Approx 14 meters (128yds) of ribbon

SPECIAL ABBREVIATIONS
ch 4 (chain 4) knit next st, * slip st back onto left-hand needle and knit it again; rep from * twice more, leaving st on right-hand needle cont on.

PATTERN REPEAT

Row 1 (RS) K1, * k1, ch 4, k7, ch 4; rep from * 9 times, k2.
Row 2 (and every WS row) P93 sts.
Row 3 * K3, ch 4, k5, ch 4; rep from * 9 times, k3.
Row 5 K1, * k3, ch 4, k3, ch 4, k2; rep from * 9 times, k2.
Row 7 K1, * k4, ch 4, k1, ch 4, k3; rep from * 9 times, k2.
Row 9 K1, * k5, ch 4, k4; rep from * 9 times, k2.
Row 11 As row 7.
Row 13 As row 5.
Row 15 As row 3.
Row 17 As row 1.
Row 19 K1, * ch 4, k9; rep from * 9 times, ch 4, k1.
Row 20 P93 sts.
These 20 rows form pattern repeat.

BLANKET

Using 4.50mm (US 7) needles, cast on 139 sts.
Row 1 (RS) K1, * p1, k1; rep from * to end.
Row 2 As row 1.
These 2 rows form Moss st pattern.
Cont working in Moss st for 10cm (4in), ending on a WS row.
(RS) Moss st 23 sts, k93 sts, Moss st to end.
(WS) Moss st 23 sts, p93 sts, Moss st to end.
Rep last 2 rows once more.

Establishment rows

(RS) Moss st 23 sts, work row 1 of pattern repeat, Moss st to end.
(WS) Moss st 23 sts, work row 2 of pattern repeat, Moss st to end.
These 2 rows set pattern.
Cont working in pattern as set until 8 full repeats have been worked. (160 rows)
Now work rows 1–18 once more. (178 rows)
(RS) Moss st 23 sts, k93 sts, Moss st to end.
(WS) Moss st 23 sts, p93 sts, Moss st to end.
Rep last 2 rows once more.
Work a further 10cm (4in) in Moss st.
Cast off.
Press using a warm iron over a damp cloth.

Embroider rosebuds to center of every diamond.
Thread lengths of ribbon through diagonal spaces of the pattern, weaving in and out at regular intervals.
Secure ends. For embroidery stitch refer to page 147. ❏

Create this delightful Rosebud Crib blanket. . . it will become a treasured heirloom.

TWEED STITCH BLANKET

Worked in a simple Tweed stitch pattern, this blanket is worked in strips then, sewn together.

YARN	Ella Rae CLASSIC	
100g/3.5oz	200m/219yds	
Col.	No.	Quantity x 100g balls
col A	73	2
col B	55	2
col C	6	2

MEASUREMENTS
Width approx 60cm (23½in)
Length approx 96cm (37¾in)
NEEDLES
1 pair 4.50mm (US 7) needles.
1 embroidery needle.

TENSION/GAUGE
25 sts and 36 rows measured over 10cm of Tweed st using 4.50mm (US 7) needles.

TWEED ST

Row 1 (RS) K1, * yf, sl 1 p/wise, yb, k1; rep from * to end.
Row 2 P2, * yb, sl 1 p/wise, yf, p1; rep from * to last st, p1.
These 2 rows form pattern repeat.

BLANKET

Panel 1
Using 4.50mm (US 7) needles and col A, cast on 41 sts.
Work 15cm (6in) in Tweed St, ending on a WS row.
Change to col B, work a further 15cm (6in), ending on a WS row.
Change to col C, work a further 15cm (6in), ending on a WS row.
Change to col A, work a further 15cm (6in), ending on a WS row.
Cast off.

Panel 2
Work as for Panel 1, cast on in col B.
Work 15cm (6in) col B, 15cm (6in) col C, 15cm (6in) col A, 15cm (6in) col B.

Panel 3
Work as for Panel 1, cast on in col C.
Work 15cm (6in) in col C, 15cm (6in) in col A, 15cm (6in) in col B, 15cm (6in) in col C.

Panel 4
Work as for Panel 1.

Panel 5
Work as for Panel 2.

Panel 6
Work as for Panel 3.
Press pieces using a warm iron over a damp cloth.
Sew panels together in sequence, using edge to edge st.
(or method preferred)
Blanket st around every square using same col thread.
Embroider flower motif in center of each square, using photo as a guide. See page 147 for embroidery stitch. ❏

Do you remember your first teddy bear? I loved my "Patch" to pieces, Mom stitched him back together and eventually he was all patches, but I just could not part with him.

CROCHET BABY BLANKET

This crochet blanket is a stunning mix of beautiful, bright colors.

YARN Ella Rae CLASSIC		
100g/3.5oz	200m/219yds	
Col.	No.	Quantity x 100g balls
col 1	12	1
col 2	35	1
col 3	05	1
col 4	36	1
col 5	29	1
MC	07	1

MEASUREMENTS
Width approx 65cm (25½in)
Length approx 90cm (35½in)
Each square measures 9.5cm (3¾in)
NEEDLES
1 4.50mm (US G) crochet hook.
CROCHET ABBREVIATIONS
Refer to page 151

BLANKET

Using Col 1 make a loop. Ch 5. Join with sl st to form a ring.

1st round Cont in Col 1. Ch 2, work 11 ht in ring.
Change to col 2, join with sl st to top of ch 2 (12 ht, counting ch 2 as 1 ht).

2nd round Cont in col 2. Pull up a lp on hook approx 1.5 cm high, yo, insert hook in same st as sl st, yo, draw up a lp * (yo, insert hook in same st, yo, draw up a lp) twice (7 lps on hook), yo draw through all lps on hook, ch 1 (cluster made); yo, insert hook in next ht, yo draw up a lp. * Repeat from * to * 11 times more, omitting "yo, insert hook in next ht, yo draw up lp" after last cluster and ending ch 1, sl st to top of first cluster (12 clusters).

3rd round Change to col 3. Sl st in first sp between clusters, ch 2, ht in same sp (half of corner made), * (1 ht in top of next cluster, 1 ht in next sp) twice; 1 ht in next cluster; work 2 ht ch 2 and 2 ht in next sp (corner made). Repeat from * twice more; 1 ht in top of next cluster, 1 ht in next sp) twice; 1 ht in next cluster; ending 2 ht in first sp, ch 2 sl st to top of ch-2 (9 ht on each side and 4 corner sps).

4th round: Change to col 4. Turn. Sl st to center of first sp, draw up a lp approx 1.5cm (½in) high and work a 7-lp cluster in same sp (half of corner made), * sk 2 ht, 1 cluster in next sp) 4 times; sk 1 ht, work 1 cluster, ch 3 and 1 cluster in corner sp). Repeat from * twice more; (sk 2 ht, 1 cluster in next sp) 4 times; ending 1 cluster in first sp, ch 3, sl st to top of first cluster (6 clusters on each side and 4 corner sps).

5th round: Change col 5. Turn, ch 2 work 1 ht, ch 3 and 2 ht in corner sp, * (2 ht between next 2 clusters) 5 times; work 2 ht, ch 3 and 2 ht in next sp. Repeat from * twice more, ending (2 ht between next 2 clusters) 5 times; sl st to top of ch 2. Break off.

Make 30 squares as detailed above. Alternate cols 1–4 in each square—always use col 5 for round 5.

Joining Instructions

With RS facing, using MC, sl st in corner of a square, ch 3, tr in each st across to next corner. Break off. Work across adjoining square in same manner. Hold squares right sides together and joining edges matching. With yarn and tapestry needle, whipstitch pieces together, working through outer lp of each st. (2 small ridges formed by unworked lps on right side) Break off.

Join blocks into strips 5 blocks long using above method. Join strips using same method, to make blanket 5 x 6 blocks. With RS facing, work one row of tr around whole blanket.

Scalloped edge

With RS facing, using MC, insert hook in corner, * sk 2 sts, work 3 tr, 3 dtr and 3 tr in next st, sk 2 sts, 1dc in next st. Repeat from * around blanket, sl st-ing and adjusting for corners. ❏

Like a box of jewels, this blanket
is a treasure to behold.

MOLLY THE DOLLY

This cute felted doll will become a girl's best friend.

YARN Ella Rae CLASSIC 100g/3.5oz 200m/219yds			NEEDLES 1 pair 4.50mm (US 7) needles.	ADDITIONAL REQUIREMENTS 1 darning needle.
Col.	No.	Quantity x 100g balls	TENSION/GAUGE	Polyester Fiberfill.
col A	06	1	20 sts and 24 rows measured	Embroidery thread.
col B	30	1	over 10cm (4in) of St st using	
col C	07	1	4.50mm (US 7) needles.	
MEASUREMENTS				
Height approx 38cm (15in)				

BODY

To make body, refer to pattern page on 106.

CLOTHES

Pants (make 2)

Using 4.50mm (US 7) needles and col B, cast on 12 sts. Knit 2 rows.

Change to col C, k 1 row, p 1 row.

Change to col B, k1 row, p 1 row.

Repeat last 4 rows, 4 times, then work 2 more rows in col B. Break off yarn and hold at end of needle.

Make other leg the same.

Using col C, k across sts of both legs. (24 sts) P 1 row.

Change to col B, k 1 row, p 1 row.

Change to col C, k 1 row, p 1 row.

Repeat last 4 rows, once more, then work 8 rows in col B. Cast off.

Pinafore Dress (make 2)

Using 4.50mm (US 7) needles and col B, cast on 32 sts. Knit 2 rows.

Dec 1 st each end next row, then on foll 4th rows until 18 sts rem.

Cont working straight until length measures 12cm (4¾in) from beg, ending on a WS row.

Next row (RS) Cast off 2 sts at beg next 2 rows. (14 sts)

Next row (RS) (dec) K2tog, k to last 2 sts, k2tog. Purl 1 row.

Repeat last 2 rows, twice more. (8 sts)

Next row(RS) K3, turn, leave rem sts on a holder. St st 5 rows. Cast off.

With RS facing, rejoin yarn to rem sts, cast off 2 center sts, k to end.

St st 5 rows. Cast off.

Sweater

Back and Front (make 2)

Using 4.50mm (US 7) needles and col C, cast on 20 sts. Knit 2 rows.

Cont working in St st until length measures 8cm (3¼in), ending on a WS row.

Cast off 2 sts at beg next 2 rows.

Cont working in St st until length measures

11cm (4½in), ending on a WS row. Cast off.

Sleeves (make 2)

Using 4.50mm (US 7) needles and col C, cast on 14 sts. Knit 2 rows.

Cont working in St st until length measures 12cm (4¾in), ending on a WS row. Cast off.

Felt all pieces separately using method on page 152.

Sew side seams and shoulders of pinafore. Sew seams of pants tog.

Sew sweater sleeve and side seams. Center sleeves and join.

Embroider flower onto pinafore, using photo detail as a guide.

Embroider eyes and mouth, using photo as a guide.

Hair Cut 9 strands of yarn, approx 8cm (3¼in) in length.

Fold in half and sew fold to head of doll along seam.

Cont in this way until head is sufficiently covered. ❏

Handy Tip

Distributing the stuffing evenly throughout the toy can be difficult, especially getting into narrow spaces such as arms and legs. Use the point of a knitting needle or the blunt end of a pencil to push the polyester fiberfill into tight spaces.

CABLE AND RIB TOGGLE JACKET

A simple cable and rib jacket with wide bands and toggles.

<table>
<tr><td colspan="4">YARN Ella Rae CLASSIC
100g/3.5oz 200m/219yds</td></tr>
<tr><td></td><td>A</td><td>B</td><td>C</td></tr>
<tr><td></td><td>5–6</td><td>7–8</td><td>9–10 yrs</td></tr>
<tr><td>Chest</td><td>66</td><td>71</td><td>76 cm</td></tr>
<tr><td colspan="4">Col. No. Quantity x 100g balls</td></tr>
<tr><td>30</td><td>5</td><td>6</td><td>6</td></tr>
</table>

MEASUREMENTS
Refer to diagram on page 148.

NEEDLES
1 pair 4.00mm (US 6) needles.
1 pair 4.50mm (US 7) needles.
1 pair 4.00mm (US 6) double-ended needles.

TENSION/GAUGE
22 sts and 32 rows measured over 10cm (4in) of pattern using 4.50mm (US 7) needles.

ADDITIONAL REQUIREMENTS
3 Toggles

SPECIAL ABBREVIATIONS
C2B (Cross 2 back) knit into back of 2nd st on needle, then first st, slipping both sts off needle at same time.

Rib Pattern

Row 1 (RS) P4,* yb, sl2 p/wise, C2B, p4; rep from * to end.
Row 2 K4,* yf, sl 2 p/wise, p 2nd st on left-hand needle, then 1st st, slip both sts off needle tog, k4; rep from * to end.
Row 3 Knit.
Row 4 Purl.
Repeat these 4 rows for Rib pattern.

BACK

Using 4.50mm (US 7) needles, cast on 83(93,107) sts.
Work 3cm (1¼in) in k1, p1 rib, ending on a WS row, inc 1 st. [84(94,108) sts]
Cont working in Rib patt until length (incl band) measures 43(48,53) cm [17(19,20¾) in], ending on a WS row.
Shape shoulders (RS) Cast off 8(9,11) sts at beg next 4 rows, then 8(9,12) sts beg next 2 rows. Leave rem 36(40,40) sts on a holder.

LEFT FRONT

Using 4.50mm (US 7) needles, cast on 35(39,43) sts.
Work in k1, p1 rib for 3cm (1¼in), ending on a WS row, inc 1 st. [36(40,44) sts] **
Cont working in patt as foll:
Row 1 (RS) P4, * yb, sl2 p/wise, C2B, p4; rep from * 4(4,5) times, size B only: yb, sl2 p/wise, C2B.
Row 2 K4(0,4), * yf, sl2 p/wise, p 2nd st on left-hand needle, then 1st st, slip both sts off needle tog, k4; rep from * to end.
Row 3 Knit.
Row 4 Purl.
Rep these 4 rows.
Cont working in repeat as set, until length (incl band) measures 40(45,50) cm [13¾(17¾,19½) in], ending on a RS row.
Shape neck (WS) Cast off 3(3,2) sts at beg (neck edge) next row, then at neck edge foll alt row once, then 1 st at neck edge every foll row, 6(7,6) times.
Work 2(1,2) row/s.

Shape shoulder (RS) Cast off 8(9,11) sts at beg next row, then on foll alt row, once.
Patt 1 row. Cast off rem 8(9,12) sts.

RIGHT FRONT

Work as for left front to **.
Cont working in patt as foll: Sizes A & C work as for left front.
Size B:
Row 1 (RS) * yb, sl2 p/wise, C2B, p4; rep from * to end.
Row 2 K4 * yf, sl2 p/wise, p 2nd st on left-hand needle, then 1st st, slip both sts off needle tog, k4; rep from * to end.
Row 3 Knit.
Row 4 Purl.
Rep these 4 rows.
Cont working in repeat as set, until length (incl band) measures 40(45,50) cm [13¾(17¾,19½) in], ending on a WS row.
Shape neck (RS) Cast off 3(3,2) sts at beg (neck edge) next row, then at neck edge foll alt row once, then 1 st at neck edge every foll row, 6(7,6) times.
Work 2(1,2) row/s.
Shape shoulder (WS) Cast off 8(9,11) sts at beg next row, then on foll alt row, once.
Patt 1 row. Cast off rem 8(9,12) sts.

SLEEVES

Using 4.50mm (US 7) needles, cast on 52 sts.
Work in k1, p1 rib for 3 cm, ending on a WS row.
Cont working in rib pattern, AT THE SAME TIME shape sides as foll, working incs into pattern at sides: Inc 1 st each end every 5th row, 16(20,23) times.
Cont working straight until length (incl band) measures 31(36,41) cm [12¼(14¼,16) in], ending on a WS row. Cast off.

MAKING UP

Press pieces gently on WS, using a warm iron over a damp cloth. Join shoulder seams. Center sleeves and join. Sew side and sleeve seams.

Front bands With RS facing, using 4.00mm (US 6) needles, pickup and knit 105(117,129) sts evenly along right front edge.

Next row (WS) P1, k1; rep to end.

(RS) K1, p1; rep to end.

Cont working in rib until band measures 6cm (2¼in), ending on a WS row. Cast off in rib.

Work same for left band.

Collar With RS facing, using 4.00mm (US 6) needles, beg at center of right front band, pickup and knit 27 sts to shoulder, 36(40,40) sts from holder at back, 28 sts from shoulder to center left front band. [91(95,95) sts]

Next row (WS) P1, k1; rep to end.

(RS) K1, p1; rep to end.

Cont working in rib for 3cm (1¼in), ending on a WS row. Change to 4.50mm (US 7) needles, cont working until length measures 10cm (4in). Cast off in rib.

Toggle Loop Using 4mm double ended needles, cast on 4 sts. *K4, do not turn work, slide sts to right end of needle and pull yarn to tighten. Rep from * until cord measures 7cm (2¾in). Leave sts on needle. On same needle, pickup 4 sts from cast on edge. (8 sts).

Work in Moss st as foll:

(RS) [K1, p1] 4 times.

(WS) [p1, k1] 4 times.

Rep last 2 rows once more, then RS row again. Cast off. Sew loops to left front and toggles to right front. ❏

Handy Tip

Take care to make up your project neatly for a professional look. If ironing is required, always do this on the wrong side using a damp cloth between the iron and the work being pressed.

Where strength in the seams is required, as on toys that get a lot of handling, join the pieces together using backstitch.

128

132

129

138

130

142

140

133

136

It's the Weekend

Leave the working week behind and indulge yourself in some "me" time. Make a trip to your local farmers' markets or take in a spot of leisurely shopping. Enjoy a Sunday picnic with family and friends. It's time to relax and enjoy. Grab your hat, scarf and bag—it's the weekend.

Shopping Bag & Twisted Scarf

Whether you're off to the Saturday farmers' market, shopping, or taking a picnic on a lazy Sunday, take time to relax ~ it's the weekend!

SHOPPING BAG

Both fun and functional, this little shopping bag will get lots of use.

YARN Ella Rae CLASSIC SUPERWASH
100g/3.5oz   200m/219yds

Col.	No.	Quantity x 100g balls
col A	20	1
col B	26	1
col C	18	1
col D	15	1

NEEDLES
1 pair 4.50mm (US 7) needles.

MEASUREMENTS
Width approx 23cm (9in)
Height approx 30cm (11¾in)
Depth approx 5cm (2in)
TENSION/GAUGE
16 sts and 26 rows measured over 10cm (4in) of pattern using 4.50mm (US 7) needles.
ADDITIONAL REQUIREMENTS
1 pair bag handles.

Herringbone St Pattern

Row 1 (RS) K1 * sl 1, k1, psso but instead of dropping slipped st from left-hand needle, k into the back of it; rep from * to last st, k1.

Row 2 * P2tog, then p first st again slipping both sts off needle tog; rep from * rep from * to end.

These 2 rows form patt rep.

Color Sequence

Work 2 rows col A, 2 rows col B, 2 rows col C, 2 rows col D, 2 rows col B, 2 rows col A, 2 rows col D, 2 rows col C.

BAG

Sides (make 2)

Using 4.50mm (US 7) needles and col A, cast on 78 sts.

Cont working in patt rep and color sequence until length measures 30cm (11¾in), ending on a WS row.

Using col A, cast off 25 sts at beg next 2 rows. (28 sts)

Cont working in St st and col A until length measures 36cm (14¼in) from beg, ending on a WS row. Cast off.

Gusset (make 2)

Using 4.50mm (US 7) needles and col A, cast on 16 sts.

Cont working in patt rep until length measures same as side edge of front and back pieces [approx 30cm (11¾in)]. Cast off.

Make second piece to match.

Base

Using 4.50mm (US 7) needles and col A, cast on 16 sts.

Cont working in patt rep until length measures same as cast on edge of front and back pieces [approx 28cm (11in)]. Cast off.

MAKING UP

Edge to edge st is used to sew all pieces tog (see method on page 151).

Sew side pieces tog (piece 1), alternating colors.

Press pieces gently, using a warm iron over a damp cloth.

Lay front and back pieces one on top of the other so that WS are tog. Sew each gusset piece to either side of front and back pieces, using edge to edge st (or preferred method). Sew base the same way to front and back, the sew either end to gusset at side.

Sew handles to top edge, folding extra length of front and back pieces over each handle to form a casing and slip st to inside to secure. ❏

TWISTED SCARF

This is a stunning scarf that will not fail to impress.

YARN Ella Rae CLASSIC SUPERWASH
100g/3.5oz   200m/219yds

Col. No.	Quantity x 100g balls
26	3

MEASUREMENTS
Width approx 13cm (5in)
Length appox 150cm (59in)
NEEDLES
1 pair 4.50mm (US 7) needles.

TENSION/GAUGE
20 sts and 36 rows measured over 10cm (4in) of Garter st using 4.50mm (US 7) needles.
SPECIAL ABBREVIATIONS
Wrap and turn—sl next st onto right-hand needle, yf, return sl st to left-hand needle, yb (wrapping yarn around sl st), turn work.
Knit wrap and wrapped st tog—Insert tip of needle under the wrap as if to knit, then into the wrapped st and k both loops tog.

SCARF

Using 4.50mm (US 7) needles,
cast on 24 sts.
Knit 2 rows.
* **Row 1** (RS) K20, wrap and turn.
Row 2 (WS) Knit.
Row 3 K16, wrap and turn.
Row 4 Knit.
Row 5 K12, wrap and turn.
Row 6 Knit.
Row 7 K8, wrap and turn.
Row 8 Knit.
Row 9 K4, wrap and turn.
Row 10 Knit.
Row 11 K across all 24 sts,
knitting wrap and wrapped st tog.
Row 12 Knit. **
These 12 rows form patt rep.
Cont working in repeat from * to ** until
length measures approx 150cm (59in),
ending on a row 12 of patt rep.
Knit 2 rows. Cast off. ❏

FELTED HAT

This gorgeous hat is sure to turn heads. Add your own embellishments.

YARN Ella Rae CLASSIC
100g/3.5oz 200m/219yds
Col. No. **Quantity x 100g balls**
39 2
MEASUREMENTS
To fit an average size head.
NEEDLES
1 pair 8.00mm (US 11) needles.

1 set 8.00mm (US 11) double-pointed needles.
TENSION/GAUGE
12 sts and 16 rows measured over 10cm (4in)
of St st using 8.00mm (US 11) needles.
ADDITIONAL REQUIREMENTS
Ribbon.
NOTE
The hat can be shaped to fit after felting.

HAT

Crown Using 8.00mm (US 11) needles and 2 strands of yarn, cast on 6 sts.
Knit 1 row.
Purl 1 row.
Next row (RS)(inc) Inc 1 st each end next row, then 1 st each end foll alt row once more. (10 sts)
St st 7 rows.
Next row (RS) (dec) Dec 1 st each end next row, then 1 st each end foll alt row once more. (6 sts)
Purl 1 row.
Cast off.
With RS facing, using 8.00mm (US 11) double pointed needles, pickup and knit 43 sts evenly around edge of crown, place a marker.
Knit 1 round.
Next rnd (inc) * Inc 1 st, k4; rep from * to last 3 sts, inc 1 st, k2. (52 sts)
Knit 1 round.

Next rnd (inc) * Inc 1 st, k5; rep from * to last 4 sts, inc 1 st, k3. (61 sts)
Knit 1 round.
Next rnd (inc) * Inc 1 st, k6; rep from * to last 5 sts, inc 1 st, k4. (70 sts)
Knit 30 rounds.
Brim Next rnd (inc) * Inc 1 st, k1; rep from * to end. (105 sts)
Knit 5 rounds.
Next rnd (inc) * K4, inc 1 st; rep from * to end. (126 sts)
Cont working in rounds of knit until brim length measures 19cm (7½in).
Cast off.
Darn in all loose ends.
Felt using method on page 152.
Stretch into shape while still damp. ❏

Handy Tip

Personalize your hat by adding your own embellishments — a gorgeous brooch, velvet ribbon or a floral display.

STRIPED SCARF

This scarf is worked lengthwise. The strong vertical stripes are its distinguishing feature.

YARN Ella Rae CLASSIC SUPERWASH
100g/3.5oz   200m/219yds

Col. No.	Quantity x 100g balls
col A 20	1
col B 32	1
col C 18	1

MEASUREMENTS (without fringe)
Width approx 13cm (5in)
Length approx 160cm (63in)

NEEDLES
1 set 6.50mm (US 10½) long circular needles.

TENSION/GAUGE
23 sts and 26 rows measured over 10cm (4in) of patt using 6.50mm (US 10½) needles.

NOTE
A circular needle is used for length, the scarf is knitted in rows not rounds.

SCARF

Using 6.50mm (US 10½) circular needles and col A,
cast on 345 sts.
(RS) K1 * yf, sl 1 p/wise, yb, k1; rep from * to end.
(WS) P2 * yb, sl 1p/wise, yf, p1; rep from * to last st, p1.
Rep these 2 rows throughout.

Cont working in pattern repeat AT THE SAME TIME work in color sequence as foll:
Work 6 rows col A, * 4 rows col B, 4 rows col C, 4 rows col B, 6 rows col A; rep from * once more.
Cast off.

FRINGE

Cut strands of yarn 20cm (8 in) in length in all colors.
Take 1 strand of each color, fold strands in half. Insert a crochet hook just above cast on edge from back to front.
Catch the folded strands of yarn with the hook and pull through the knitting. Insert the ends of yarn into the loop and pull through to tighten.
Cont in this way until edge is sufficiently covered with fringes.
Repeat at other end. ❏

Handy Tip

Circular needles sometimes get kinks or curls in the plastic or nylon section. To remove these, immerse the needle in hot water and stretch back into shape.

TRAVEL WRAP

*A versatile travel wrap is
a must for every home.
Worked in an easy pattern
and machine washable wool.*

YARN Ella Rae CLASSIC SUPERWASH	**NEEDLES**
100g/3.5oz 200m/219yds	1 pair 5.00mm (US 8) needles.
Col. No. Quantity x 100g balls	**TENSION/GAUGE**
22 10	20 sts and 24 rows measured over 10cm (4in)
MEASUREMENTS	of St st using 5.00mm (US 8) needles.
Width approx 120cm (42¼in)	**SPECIAL ABBREVIATION**
Length approx 150cm (59in)	M1 (make 1) pick up st lying between st just
	worked and next st and knit into it.

Pattern Repeat

Row 1 (WS) K4, p to last 4 sts, k4.
Row 2 (RS) K4, * sl 1, k1, psso, m1;
rep from * to last st, k4.
Row 3 K4, p to last 4 sts, k4.
Row 4 K4, * m1, k2tog; rep from * to last st, k4.
These 4 rows form pattern repeat.

THROW

Using 5.00mm (US 8) needles, cast on 200 sts.
Knit 5 rows.
Cont working in pattern repeat until length
measures 150cm (59in), ending on a RS row.
Knit 5 rows.
Cast off.

Press gently, using a warm iron over a damp cloth. ❏

Handy Tip

*To fix a mistake, the same method
applies as for a dropped stitch.
Drop the stitch immediately above
the mistake (even if it is some rows
down), forming a ladder down to it.
Using a crochet hook, pick up all the
stitches back up the ladder to the
row being worked.*

Create a travel wrap to take with you . . . it will hold your special memories for years to come.

Travel Wrap

BOBBLE THROW

This is a stunning throw made up of triangles that are sewn together to form squares, and then the squares sewn to make up the throw.

YARN Ella Rae CLASSIC SUPERWASH
100g/3.5oz 200m/219yds

Col. No.   Quantity x 100g balls
36   14

MEASUREMENTS
Width approx 110cm (43¼in)
Length approx 155cm (61in)

NEEDLES
1 pair 4.50mm (US 7) needles.

TENSION/GAUGE
20 sts and 24 rows measured over 10cm (4in) of St st using 4.50mm (US 7) needles.

SPECIAL ABBREVIATIONS
B1 Knit into the front, then back of same st.
B1p Purl into the back, then front of same st.
MB1 [k1, p1, k1, p1, k1, p1] all into next st, turn, k6, turn, p6, pass 2nd, 3rd, 4th, 5th and 6th sts over 1st st one st at a time. (bobble complete)
MB2 [k1, p1, k1, p1, k1, p1] all into next st, pass 2nd, 3rd, 4th, 5th and 6th sts over 1st st one st at a time. (bobble complete)

THROW

Triangle (4 triangles make 1 square)
Using 4.50mm (US 7) needles,
cast on 1 st.
Row 1 B1 (2 sts)
Row 2 K1, B1 (3 sts)
Row 3 K2, B1 (4 sts)
Row 4 K3, B1 (5 sts)
Row 5 K2, MB1, k1, B1 (6 sts)
Row 6–12 K to last st, B1 (13 sts)
Row 13 K12, B1 (14 sts)
Row 14 * K1, sl 1 p/wise; rep from * to last 2 sts, k1, B1 (15 sts)
Row 15 K14, B1 (16 sts)
Row 16 K2, * sl 1 p/wise, k1; rep from * to last 2 sts, sl 1 p/wise, B1 (17 sts)
Row 17 K16, B1 (18 sts)
Row 18 As row 14 (19 sts)
Row 19 K18, B1 (20 sts)
Row 20 As row 16 (21 sts)
Row 21 K20, B1 (22 sts)
Row 22 As row 14 (23 sts)
Row 23 K22, B1 (24 sts)
Row 24 As row 16 (25 sts)
Row 25 K24, B1 (26 sts)
Row 26 K25, B1 (27 sts)
Row 27 K26, B1 (28 sts)
Row 28 K27, B1 (29 sts)
Row 29 K28, B1 (30 sts)
Row 30 K29, B1 (31 sts)
Row 31 K30, B1 (32 sts)
Row 32 P31, B1p (33 sts)
Row 33 K32, B1 (34 sts)
Row 34 K33, B1 (35 sts)
Row 35 K2, [yf,k2tog] 16 times, B1 (36 sts)
Row 36 K35, B1 (37 sts)
Row 37 K36, B1 (38 sts)
Row 38 P37, B1p (39 sts)
Row 39 K2, [MB2,k4] 7 times, MB2, B1 (40 sts)
Row 40 P39, B1p (41 sts)
Row 41 K40, B1 (42 sts)
Row 42 K41, B1 (43 sts)
Row 43 K2, [yf,k2tog] 20 times,B1 (44 sts)
Row 44 K43, B1 (45 sts)
Row 45 K44, B1 (46 sts)
Row 46 P45, B1p (47 sts)
Row 47 K46, B1 (48 sts)
Row 48 K47, B1 (49 sts)
Row 49 K48, B1 (50 sts)
Row 50 K49, B1 (51 sts)
Row 51 K50, B1 (52 sts)
Row 52 K51, B1 (53 sts)
Row 53 Cast off.

Make a total of 80 triangles.
Sew 4 triangles together to make a square (20 squares)
Sew squares together,
4 wide by 5 rows.
Press gently, using a warm iron over a damp cloth. ❏

Pick a blanket and take a picnic.

CHEVRON AFGHAN

*Worked in strips and a
beautiful mix of colors,
this project is great for
using up scraps of yarn.*

YARN Ella Rae AMITY			MEASUREMENTS
100g/3.5oz 200m/219yds			Width approx 120cm (42¼in)
Col.	No.	Quantity x 100g balls	Length approx 150cm (59in)
col A	112	3	NEEDLES
col B	25	3	1 pair 5.00mm (US 8) needles.
col C	21	3	TENSION/GAUGE
col D	23	3	18 sts and 24 rows measured over
col E	31	3	10cm (4in) of St st using 5.00mm (US 8) needles.
col F	9	3	

Pattern Repeat

Row 1 (RS) K1, sl 1, k1, psso, k9, sl 2, k1,
p2sso, k9, k2tog, k1.
Row 2 K1, * p1, k4, (k1, yf, k1) all into
next st, k4; rep from * once more, p1, k1.
These 2 rows form pattern repeat.

THROW

Strip 1

Using 5.00mm (US 8) needles and col A,
cast on 27 sts.
Knit 1 row.
Cont working in pattern repeat as foll:
* work 4 rows col A, 2 rows col B,
4 rows col A, 2 rows col C,
4 rows col D, 2 rows col E,
4 rows col D, 2 rows col F,
4 rows col B, 2 rows col A,
4 rows col B, 2 rows col D,
4 rows col C, 2 rows col E,
4 rows col C, 2 rows col F,
4 rows col E, 2 rows col B,
4 rows col E, 2 rows col C,
4 rows col F, 2 rows col A,
4 rows col F, 2 rows col D **;
rep from * to ** 4 times more, then
work 4 rows col A, 2 rows col B,
4 rows col A. Cast off.

Strip 2

Using 5.00mm (US 8) needles and col B,
cast on 27 sts.
Knit 1 row.
Cont working in pattern repeat as foll:
* work 4 rows col B, 2 rows col A,
4 rows col B, 2 rows col D,
4 rows col C, 2 rows col E,
4 rows col C, 2 rows col F,
4 rows col E, 2 rows col B,
4 rows col E, 2 rows col C,
4 rows col F, 2 rows col A,
4 rows col F, 2 rows col D,
4 rows col A, 2 rows col B,
4 rows col A, 2 rows col C,
4 rows col D, 2 rows col E,
4 rows col D, 2 rows col F **;
rep from * to ** 4 times more, then
work 4 rows col B, 2 rows col A,
4 rows col B.
Cast off.
Make 6 each of Strip 1 and Strip 2.
(12 strips made)

Sew strips together using edge to
edge st, alternating each other.
Darn in all loose ends ❑

Invest your time to create a beautiful throw,
and you will be rewarded with warmth and joy.
It will be appreciated by generations to come.

GARTER STITCH THROW

This is one of the easiest throws ever.

YARN Ella Rae AMITY			MEASUREMENTS
100g/3.5oz 200m/219yds			Width approx 90cm (35½in)
Col.	No.	Quantity x 100g balls	Length approx 128cm (50½in)
col A	19	2	NEEDLES
col B	25	2	1 pair 5.00mm (US 8) needles.
col C	31	2	TENSION/GAUGE
col D	32	2	18 sts and 24 rows measured over 10cm
col E	33	2	(4in) of St st using 5.00mm (US 8) needles.

THROW

Triangles

(4 triangles make a square)

Using 5.00mm (US 8) needles, begin with 1 st on needle.

Knit into front of st, yf, k same st. (3 sts)

Knit 1 row.

K1, yf, k to last st, yf, k1. (5 sts)

Repeat last 2 rows until 27 sts on needle.

Knit 1 row.

Cast off.

Make 36 triangles in each cols A and B,

make 40 triangles in each cols C, D, and E.

(192 triangles made)

With RS tog, using edge to edge st,

sew 4 triangles to make a square.

Rep this until all triangles are sewn into squares.

(48 squares made)

Arrange squares in random order of color,

6 squares wide to make a row.

Rep this until 8 rows are made.

Sew squares together using edge to edge st.

(or method preferred)

Press using a warm iron over a damp cloth. ❏

Your best friend will love this picnic blanket as much as you will.

GARTER STITCH DIAMOND THROW

This throw is simple to knit, but the effect of the diamonds when sewn together makes it stand out.

YARN	Ella Rae CLASSIC		MEASUREMENTS (without fringe)
100g/3.5oz	200m/219yds		Width approx 95cm (37½in)
Col. No.	Quantity x 100g balls		Length approx 100cm (39½in)
col A 15	2		NEEDLES
col B 25	2		1 pair 4.50mm (US 7) needles.
col C 74	2		TENSION/GAUGE
col D 71	3		20 sts and 24 rows measured over 10cm (4in)
			St st using 4.50mm (US 7) needles.

SQUARE (make 64)

Using 4.50mm (US 7) needles and col A, beg with 1 st on needle.

Row 1 (RS) K into front, back and front again of 1 st. (3 sts)

Row 2 Inc 1 st, k2. (4 sts)

Row 3 Inc 1 st, k to end. (5 sts)

Rep row 3 once more. (6 sts)

Change to col B, work row 3, 4 times.

Change to col C, work row 3, twice.

Change to col A, work row 3, twice.

Change to col D, work row 3, 6 times.

Change to col C, work row 3, 4 times.

Change to col B, work row 3, twice.

Change to col D, work row 3, twice.

Change to col A, work row 3, 4 times. (32 sts)

Next row (dec) Using col A, k2tog, k to end.

Rep last row 3 times. (28 sts)

Change to col D, work dec row twice.

Change to col B, work dec row twice.

Change to col C, work dec row 4 times.

Change to col D, work dec row 6 times.

Change to col A, work dec row twice.

Change to col C, work dec row twice.

Change to col B, work dec row 4 times.

Change to col A, work dec row until 1 st remains. Cast off 1 st.

Be bold with your choice of color.

Darn in all loose ends. Press pieces using a warm iron over a damp cloth.

Join 4 squares together to form large diamond square, matching colors.

Sew large diamond squares, 4 wide by 4 length.

Fringe

Using col D, make fringe by cutting strands approx 15cm (6in) long.

With WS facing, using a crochet hook and 5 strands of yarn, fold yarn in half and draw loop through a stitch along edge of throw, pull ends through loop and tighten.

Rep this along all sides of throw at regular intervals. ❏

Information and Resources

Leanne Prouse

"I believe good design is timeless—it's the combination of classic and contemporary elements that come together to create the Ella Rae collection."

Leanne Prouse,
Ella Rae designer

Handknitting has always been a part of her life, as has design, a skill handed down from generation to generation. "I was extremely fortunate to grow up in a house where things were always being created, as my mother is a talented dressmaker and knitter. My love of design meant I could have an idea, then get her to sew or knit it up for me. Although I learned basic stitches at an early age, I never had the patience for knitting at that stage—I'd much rather have spent my time sourcing and designing the next project then getting Mum to knit it! The first garment I knitted was when I was about 18. I found a design I liked in a magazine and knitted it up with no pattern to follow but using Mum for guidance."

After leaving school and studying fashion design and textiles, then spending many years traveling the world, she returned to live in the beautiful southwest coastal region of Australia, where she had grown up, to raise her own family.

As it happened, the same town was home to an established international knitwear design house. Looking for another challenge to embark on while raising a young family, she approached the designer with some design ideas. "That was a very happy and exciting time. The moment I walked into that design studio I felt like I belonged there. Being surrounded by all the yarn and amazing colors really ignited the passion for knitwear design as a career option not just a hobby." Following this initial contact, Leanne went on to become a head designer with the company.

After going out on her own in 2004, she has gone on to develop the Ella Rae label in association with KFI (Knitting Fever Inc). Ella Rae continues to grow and showcase the love of design that keeps on evolving and changing with the seasons.

FLOOR PILLOW
PATTERN PAGE 22
☐ Col No. 59 ▨ Col No. 139 ■ Col No. 46 ▨ Col No. 98

PATCHWORK THROW
PATTERN PAGE 40

Sq 1	Sq 3 col D	Sq 1	Sq 3 col A	Sq 1	Sq 3 col F	Sq 1
Sq 3 col A	Sq 4 col A	Sq 2 col F	Sq 4 col B	Sq 2 col A	Sq 2 col D	Sq 3 col F
Sq 1	Sq 2 col F	Sq 1	Sq 2 col A	Sq 1	Sq 2 col A	Sq 1
Sq 3 col F	Sq 4 col B	Sq 2 col D	Sq 4 col A	Sq 2 col F	Sq 4 col B	Sq 3 col D
Sq 1	Sq 2 col D	Sq 1	Sq 2 col F	Sq 1	Sq 2 col A	Sq 1
Sq 3 col D	Sq 4 col A	Sq 2 col D	Sq 4 col B	Sq 2 col D	Sq 4 col A	Sq 3 col F
Sq 1	Sq 2 col F	Sq 1	Sq 2 col A	Sq 1	Sq 2 col D	Sq 1
Sq 3 col A	Sq 4 col B	Sq 2 col F	Sq 4 col A	Sq 2 col F	Sq 4 col B	Sq 3 col F
Sq 1	Sq 3 col A	Sq 1	Sq 3 col A	Sq 1	Sq 3 col D	Sq 1

FELTED POUCH EMBROIDERY GUIDE
PATTERN PAGE 92

Create seven petals using Lazy Daisy Stitch

Blanket Stitch

Chain Stitch

ROSEBUD CRIB BLANKET
PATTERN PAGE 114

Create three Bullion Stitches around a French Knot

TWEED STITCH BLANKET
PATTERN PAGE 116

Create six petals using Lazy Daisy Stitch around a French Knots in the centre.

FLOOR PILLOW EMBROIDERY GUIDE
PATTERN PAGE 22

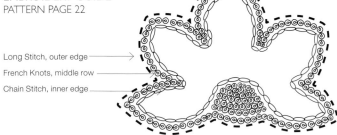

Long Stitch, outer edge

French Knots, middle row

Chain Stitch, inner edge

FELTED BABY SLIPPERS
PATTERN PAGE 102

ROLL-NECK SWEATER
PATTERN PAGE 26

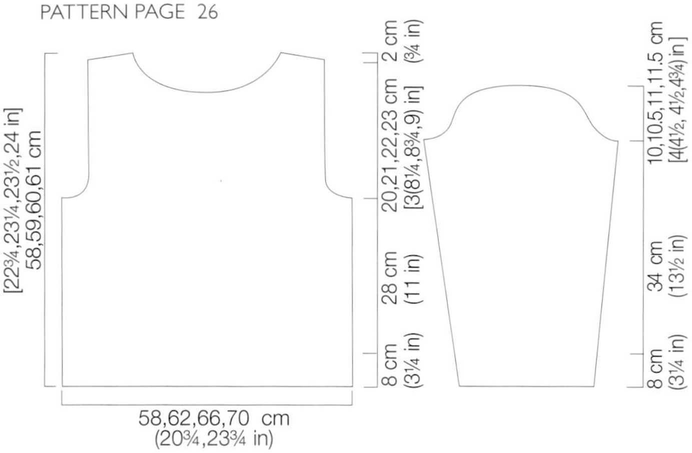
2 cm (¾ in)
20,21,22,23 cm [3(8¼,8¾,9) in]
28 cm (11 in)
8 cm (3¼ in)
58,59,60,61 cm [22¾,23¼,23½,24 in]
58,62,66,70 cm (20¾,23¾ in)
10,10.5,11,11.5 cm [4(4½, 4½,4¾) in]
34 cm (13½ in)
8 cm (3¼ in)

CABLE & DOUBLE MOSS STITCH SWEATER
PATTERN PAGE 108

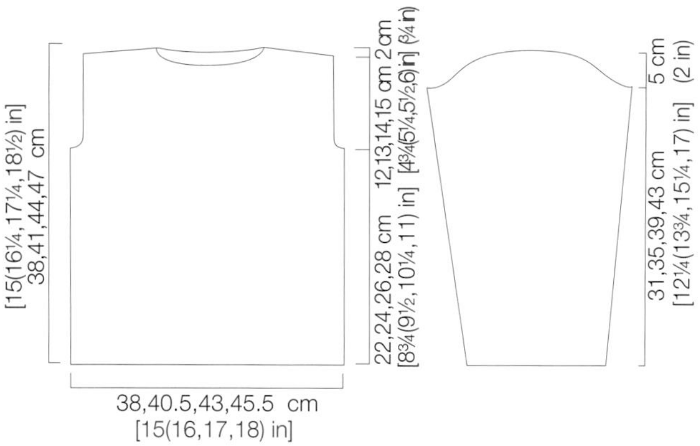
38,41,44,47 cm [15(16¼,17¼,18½) in]
2 cm (¾ in)
12,13,14,15 cm [4¾(5¼,5½,6) in]
22,24,26,28 cm [8¾(9½,10¼,11) in]
38,40.5,43,45.5 cm [15(16,17,18) in]
5 cm (2 in)
31,35,39,43 cm [12¼(13¾,15¼,17) in]

HOODED HOUSE COAT
PATTERN PAGE 30

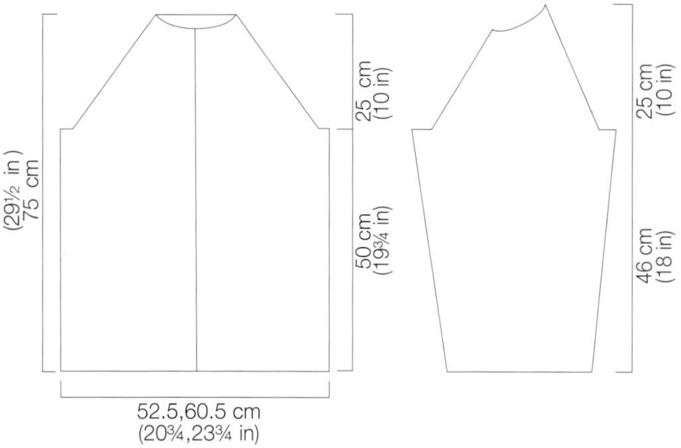
75 cm (29½ in)
25 cm (10 in)
50 cm (19¾ in)
52.5,60.5 cm (20¾,23¾ in)
25 cm (10 in)
46 cm (18 in)

CABLE AND RIB TOGGLE JACKET
PATTERN PAGE 122

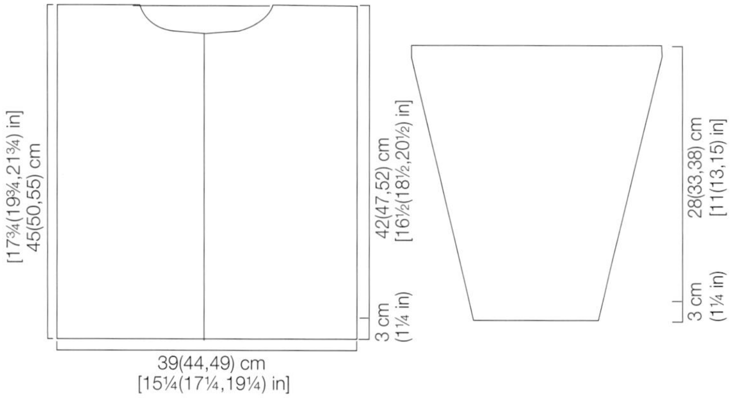
45(50,55) cm [17¾(19¾,21¾) in]
42(47,52) cm [16½(18½,20½) in]
3 cm (1¼ in)
39(44,49) cm [15¼(17¼,19¼) in]
28(33,38) cm [11(13,15) in]
3 cm (1¼ in)

CASUAL ROLL-NECK SWEATER
PATTERN PAGE 66

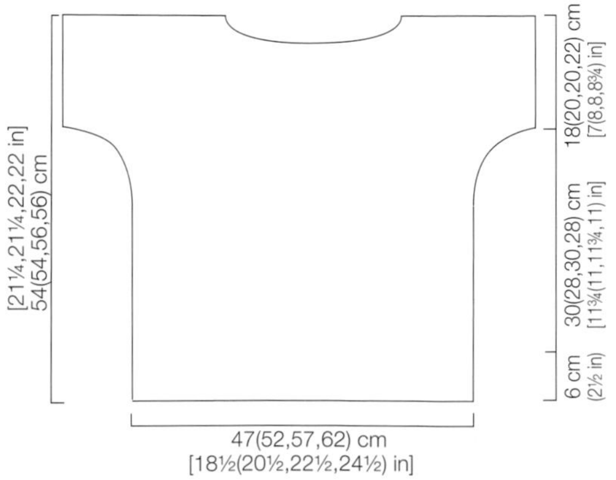
54(54,56,56) cm [21¼,21¼,22,22 in]
18(20,20,22) cm [7(8,8,8¾) in]
30(28,30,28) cm [11¾(11,11¾,11) in]
6 cm (2½ in)
47(52,57,62) cm [18½(20½,22½,24½) in]

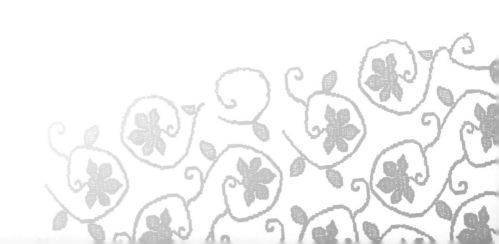

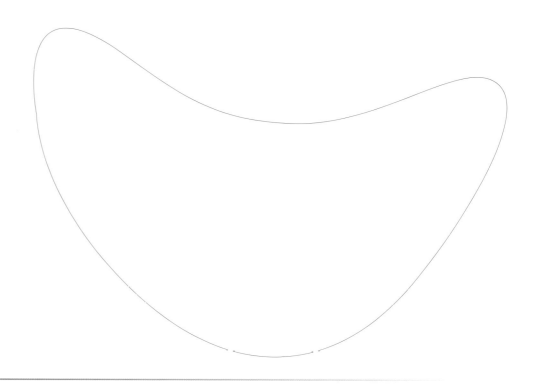

FELTED BIRD MOBILE
TEMPLATE—TO SIZE
PATTERN PAGE 14

FELTED OTTOMAN
PATTERN PAGE 45

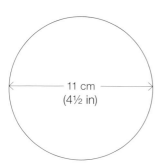

11 cm
(4½ in)

(1½ in)
4

(5¾ in)
14.5 cm

14 cm
(5½ in)

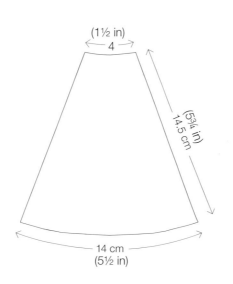

(8 in)
20 cm

15 cm
(6 in)

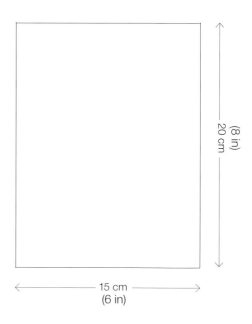

alt	alternate
beg	beginning
b	work through the back
col	color
cont	continue
cm	centimetres
cn	cable needle
circ	circular
dec	decrease
foll	following
inc	increase
incl	including
in/s	inch/es
K, k	knit
KB1	knit into back of next st
K1B	insert needle through centre of st below next st on needle and knit this in the usual way, slipping the st above off needle at same time.
mm	millimetres
m 1	make 1, pick up thread lying between sts and knit it
patt	pattern
P, p	purl
PB1	purl into back of next st
psso	pass slipped stitch over
rem	remaining
rep	repeat
rev	reverse
RS	right side
sl 1	slip one stitch
sh sh	shoulder shaping
st st	stocking stitch
st/s	stitch/es
tbl	through back of loop
tog	together
vers	version
WS	wrong side
wyif/wyib	with yarn in front or with yarn in back of stitch
yb	yarn back
yfon	yarn forward over needle
yfwd/yf	yarn forward
yon	yarn over needle
yrn	yarn around needle
yrs	years

UK/US GLOSSARY/TERMINOLOGY

Cast off = Bind off

Tension = Gauge

Stocking Stitch = Stockinette Stitch

Moss St = Seed Stitch

CROCHET ABBREVIATIONS

sl st	slip stitch
lp	loop
ch	chain
htr	half treble
sp	space
sk	skip
yo	yarn over
MC	main color
approx	approximately
dc	double crochet
tr	treble
dtr	double treble

BASIC CROCHET STITCHES

Double crochet (dc)
Insert hook into st, yo hook, draw through stitch. There are now 2 lps on hook, yo, draw through 2 lps on hook. 1 lp remains on hook. St completed.

Treble (tr)
Yo, insert hook in st, yo, draw through st. 3 lps on hook. Yo, draw through 2 lps. 2 lps remain on hook. Yo again, draw through the 2 remaining lps. 1 lp remains on hook. St completed.

Half treble (htr)
Yo, insert hook in st, yo, draw through st. 3 lps on hook. Yo, draw through all 3 lps at once. 1 lp on hook. St completed.

Double treble (dtr)
Yo twice, insert hook in st. Yo, draw lp through st. 4 lps on hook. Yo, draw through 2 lps on hook, 3 lps remain. Yo, draw through 2 lps on hook. 2 lps remain on hook. Yo, draw through remaining lps. 1 lp remains on hook. St completed.

NEEDLE CONVERSION

metric (mm)	US	UK
2	0	14
2.25	1	13
2.50	2	-
2.75	-	12
3	3	11
3.25	-	10
3.50	4	-
3.75	5	9
4	6	8
4.50	7	7
5	8	6
5.50	9	5
6	10	4
6.50	10.5	3
7	-	2
7.50	-	1
8	11	0
9	13	00
10	15	000

IMPERIAL/METRIC CONVERSION

1 in	=	2.5 cm
2 in	=	5 cm
4 in	=	10 cm
10 in	=	25.5 cm

TENSION/GAUGE

To achieve the results shown throughout the book, it is essential to work at the correct tension/gauge. This is given at the beginning of each pattern. It is important to check tension/gauge before commencing each project, as every knitter's tension/gauge varies. Using the yarn and needle size stated and working in the given stitch or pattern, knit a swatch approx 15cm (6in) square. Place the swatch on a flat surface. Measure 10cm (4in) horizontally across the center of the swatch for the stitch tension/gauge or vertically down the swatch for the row tension/gauge. Fewer stitches than stated means your work is too loose so you need to use smaller needles; more stitches than stated means your work is too tight and you need to use a bigger size needle. Continue changing needle size until the specified number of stitches is achieved (or as close to it as possible). Changing the needle size is not important as long as you obtain the correct number of stitches and rows to 10cm (4in).

FINISHING

Edge to edge st: With RS facing, align edges. Working from underneath loop of edge st on garment, draw sewing thread through this st, then st on other edge directly opposite, pull sewing thread through both sts so that they butt tog (do not pull too tightly). This gives garments an almost invisible seam that is not bulky.

Backstitch: With RS tog, sew along seam approx 1 row from edge. Insert sewing needle from back through to the front, then take thread through to back again approx 1 st to the right. Pass thread through to front again approx 2 sts to the left. Repeat this along seam. This stitch makes a strong seam; it is mainly used for shoulders and sleeves.

YARN QUANTITIES

All the designs in this book are knitted using Ella Rae yarns. The names and shades are specified at the beginning of each pattern. Different yarns may vary in thickness and therefore not knit up as you anticipate, so to avoid disappointment it is recommended not to substitute yarn if possible.

Yarn requirements are given at the beginning of each pattern and are based on average requirements so are therefore approximate. It is a good idea on larger projects to buy an extra ball of yarn, as it sometimes hard to match the correct dyelot at a later date, especially if your project has taken a few months to complete, and the store you purchased it from may have sold out.

YARN COLORS AND SUBSTITUTES

Some colors may become unavailable or your local yarn store may not hold the full range, so it may be necessary to find a similar shade or tone to the ones used throughout the book. For the patterns that require Ella Rae Classic yarn, it is possible to interchange any of the yarns from the following ranges: Ella Rae Classic, Ella Rae Classic Heathers, Ella Rae Classic Superwash.

YARNS USED IN THIS BOOK

Ella Rae CLASSIC
Worsted weight yarn   Composition: 100% Wool
4.50mm needles (US 7)
Tension/Gauge 20 sts and 24/26 rows
Yardage: 100g/3.5oz 200m/219yds

Ella Rae CLASSIC HEATHERS
Worsted weight yarn   Composition: 100% Wool
4.50mm needles (US 7)
Tension/Gauge 20 sts and 24/26 rows
Yardage: 100g/3.5oz 200m/219yds

Ella Rae CLASSIC SUPERWASH
Worsted weight yarn   Composition: 100% Superwashable Wool
4.50mm needles (US 7)
Tension/Gauge 20 sts and 24/26 rows
Yardage: 100g/3.5oz 200m/219yds

Ella Rae AMITY
Aran weight yarn   Composition: 75% Acrylic, 25% Wool
5.00mm needles (US 8)
Tension/Gauge 18 sts and 24 rows
Yardage: 100g/3.5oz 182m/200yds

WASHING It is recommended that you use a top-loading washing machine. You will need to check the progress at intervals to control the shrinkage.
Some newer models of front loaders are suitable, so long as they allow you to open the door during the wash cycle. In preparation for washing, tie off or darn any loose ends very securely to avoid them coming apart during the process.

BAGS To stop the top of the bag from "buckling" out of shape, using a yarn that will not felt (i.e. cotton, silk or synthetic yarn), sew top edges of back and front together using a slip st, taking care to only catch the very edge of the bag on each side—you want to have as little of the fabric touching as possible to avoid the risk of the two edges fusing together during the washing process. Remove this yarn after felting.
Place the knitted items in the machine and set it for a low water level, normal cycle, and hot water wash. Add a small amount of washing detergent and run through a full washing cycle, checking the progress at regular intervals to make sure it is not shrinking too much. Depending on the machine used, it may be necessary to repeat the wash/rinse cycle once more to achieve the required results. The finished item should be felted enough so that no stitch definition is visible on either side.

DRYING After the pieces have been felted, it may be necessary to stretch the pieces into shape to achieve the recommended size. Pull and stretch so that the shape is even all the way around and measurements are correct. It is quite easy to manipulate the fabric when it is still damp. It is also possible to use a hot iron on the fabric to get rid of unwanted creases or to manipulate things back into shape. Air dry thoroughly.

FINISHING Once the fabric is felted and dry, it is possible to cut the fabric without the risk of it unraveling. In some cases this may be necessary to achieve the shape or dimensions preferred.

The accessories used throughout have been obtained from good craft stores. There is also a good source of supplies online.

USA
KNITTING FEVER INC / KFI
315 BAYVIEW AVE
AMITYVILLE, NY 11701
516 546 3600 Tel
516 546 6871 Fax
www.knittingfever.com

AUSTRALIA
PRESTIGE FIBRES PTY LTD
PO BOX 39
BULLI NSW 2516
AUSTRALIA
61 (02) 4285 6669 Tel
info@prestigeyarns.com

DENMARK
UNIGARN & DESIGN
MARIENLYSTVEJ 24
8600 SILKEBORG
DENMARK
40 18 93 17

CANADA
DIAMOND YARNS
155 MARTIN ROSS AVE, UNIT 3
TORONTO, ONTARIO, M3J2L9
CANADA
416 736 6111 Tel
416 736 6112 Fax
www.diamondyarn.com

SWEDEN
MODEKNAPPEN
SMEDBERGSVAGEN 7
45535 MUNKEDAL
SWEDEN
46 (0) 524 233 10 Tel
info@modeknappen.se

This book would not have been possible without the help and contribution of the following people:

All my wonderful talented knitters: Janet Best, Gladys Dobrigh, Betty Hawkins, Gwen Howson, Mollie Perry, Kathleen Waldron, Whitney Weaver and Ann Willis. Their hard work and dedication should never be underestimated.

Acorn Photography, whose stunning photographs make the whole process all the more exciting.

A huge thank-you to Sheryl Stephens, whose graphic design expertise is second to none. Because of her commitment, passion and energy, this book is so beautiful.

My dear friends for their unfailing support: Lauren for the use of her wonderful home and hospitality, and Alex for her styling savvy, beautiful children, home, and always listening to me.

My long-suffering husband and children for putting up with my endless amount of projects and yarn taking over our home!

My dear mum, Gwen, for always being there for me. Her talents as a knitter and dressmaker started me on the road to this career, and for that I am eternally grateful.

Thank you to the team at Sixth & Spring for their support and confidence in letting us put this book together.

And finally thank-you to the team at Knitting Fever for giving me this opportunity. Jeff and Haydee, for all your hard work and enthusiasm and a special thank you to Sion for having faith in me.

DEBBIE BLISS
Design It, Knit It

Take a peek inside the designer's studio as
Debbie Bliss shares her secrets for creating
sensational knits with her lovely signature
yarns. Design It, Knit It takes you on a
comprehensive and inspirational journey
through the design process. Each chapter
offers an in-depth look at one of the four
most important elements of design—shape,
color, texture and details—and there's even
a section on designing for children. Winner
of the Independent Publishers Award's top
honors, the Gold Medal, for Craft category.

DEBBIE BLISS
Design It, Knit It, Babies

In this follow-up to the best-selling Design
It, Knit It, celebrated designer Debbie Bliss
knits up the most adorable collection of
baby wear ever. Fifteen all-new designs for
sporty sweaters, knits for preemies, special
occasion outfits and accessories showcase
Debbie's signature style and her exquisite
yarns.

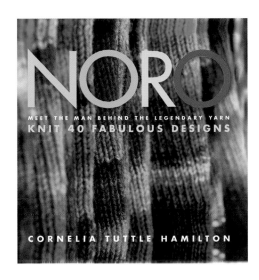

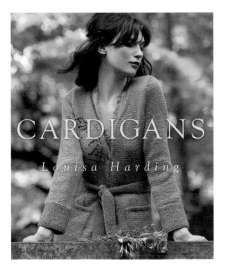

CORNELIA TUTTLE HAMILTON
NORO

Designer Cornelia Tuttle Hamilton has been working with Noro yarns for more than 25 years. In this book, she traveled to Japan to meet the enigmatic creator of these yarns and discuss his craft, his continuing commitment to sustainability and his unwavering dedication to yarn-making as an art form. Packed with color photographs and insights into the world of Noro, it features 40 stunning projects, including pullovers, cardigans, accessories and more.

LOUISA HARDING
Cardigans

Cardigans will change the way you think about this classic fashion staple. In Louisa Harding's designs, the humble cardigan is transformed with grace and beauty into dozens of unique creations. Included here are more than 25 patterns in her beautiful and versatile yarns, with variations on each pattern. More than 40 unique designs are collected here—all with accompanying full color photographs, charts and instructions.

VISIT SIXTHANDSPRINGBOOKS.COM
TO ORDER, OR CALL TOLL-FREE 877-860-6164